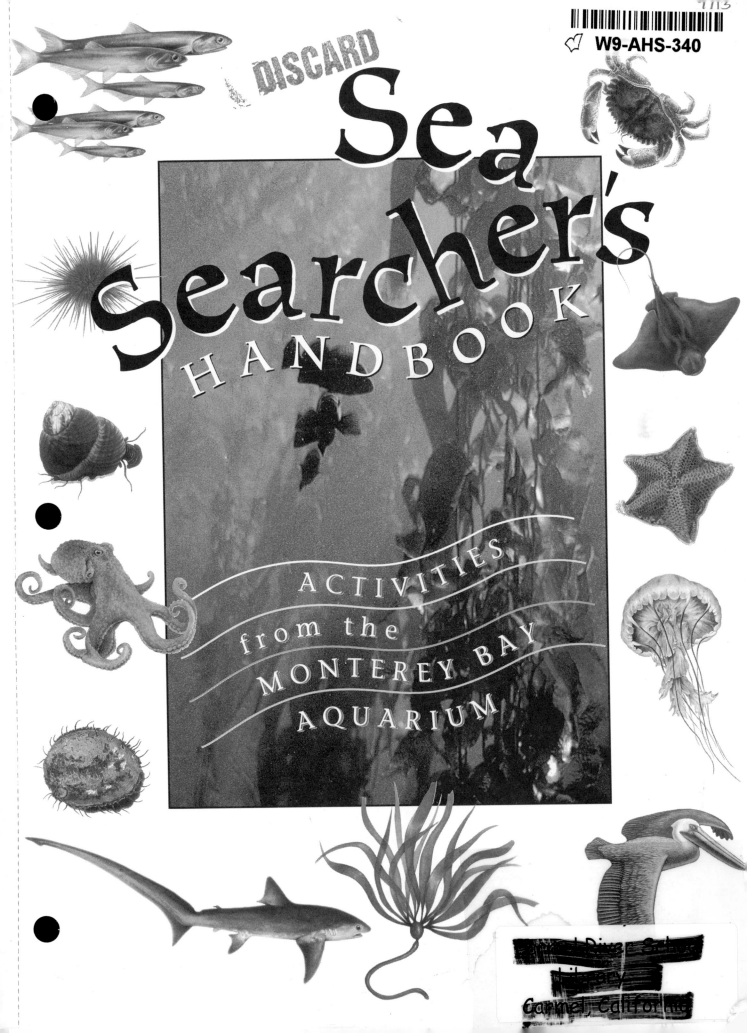

Sea Searcher's HANDBOOK

ACTIVITIES from the MONTEREY BAY AQUARIUM

MONTEREY BAY AQUARIUM®

886 CANNERY ROW
MONTEREY, CA 93940-1085
TELEPHONE (408)648-4800
FAX (408)648-4810
http://www.mbayaq.org

The purpose of the Monterey Bay Aquarium is to stimulate interest, increase knowledge and promote stewardship of the Monterey Bay and the world's ocean environment through innovative exhibits, public education and scientific research.

Printed in the United States
Published in cooperation with
ROBERTS RINEHART PUBLISHERS
5455 Spine Road, Boulder, CO 80301
(303) 530-4400

Distributed to the book trade by Publishers Group West

Library of Congress Cataloging in Publication Data

Sea searcher's handbook: activities from the Monterey Bay Aquarium/[editor, Pam Armstrong].

Includes bibliographical references.

Summary: Surveys kelp forest, wetlands, the open ocean, and other aquatic environments, encountering otters, sharks, and many more creatures.

ISBN 1-878244-15-9 (pbk.)

Marine ecology—Juvenile literature. 2. Marine animals—Juvenile literature. 3. Marine ecology—Study and teaching—Activity programs—Juvenile literature. [1. Marine animals. 2. Marine ecology 3. Ecology.] Armstrong, Pam 1961-Monterey Bay Aquarium

QH541.S3S33 1996

574.5'2636—dc20   96-27100 CIP

PROJECT MANAGER: Nora L. Deans
PROJECT EDITOR: Roxane Buck-Ezcurra
EDITOR: Pam Armstrong
DESIGNER: Ann W. Douden

PHOTO CREDITS:

Bucich, Richard: front cover

Monterey Bay Aquarium: title page, 84, 108, 202

Webster, Steven K.: 3, 173, 215

Randy, Wilder/Monterey Bay Aquarium: 216, 218 (top left), 219, 220

Credits continued on page 224.

To all the young sea searchers of the world, and to all those who open the world of nature for them to discover and preserve.

Many thanks to all the teachers, students, advisors and Monterey Bay Aquarium staff who have participated over the years in the development and use of the activities and information in this book. There is no more important nor urgent work than helping others to know, love and take care of the sea.

Special thanks go to all who have participated in researching, writing, reviewing and editing the wealth of resources contained in this book. We appreciate your support in making the wonders of the sea available for others to enjoy.

Contributing writers:

Pam Armstrong
Judith Connor
Chris Parsons
Judy Rand
Jenny Vuturo-Brady

Reviewers:

Arlene Breise
Jeff Bryant
Ann Dauben
Nora L. Deans
Andrew DeVogelaere
Linda Martin
Mike Rigsby
Pat Rutowski
Mark Silberstein
Bruce Stewart
Steven K. Webster

Many thanks to everyone else, far too numerous to list, who over the years have helped make this book possible.

Sea Searcher's Handbook

CONTENTS

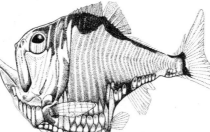

CONTENTS

CONTENTS

"A child's world is fresh and new and beautiful, full of wonder and excitement. It is our misfortune that for most of us that clear-eyed vision, that true instinct for what is beautiful and awe-inspiring, is dimmed and even lost before we reach adulthood. If I had influence with the good fairy who is supposed to preside over the christening of all children I should ask that her gift to each child in the world be a sense of wonder so indestructible that it would last throughout life, as an unfailing antidote against the boredom and disenchantments of later years, the sterile preoccupation with things that are artificial, the alienation from the sources of our strength."

RACHEL CARSON (1907–1956)

CLUES FOR SEARCHING THE SEA

School of Anchovies

Red urchin

Brown turban
snail

Red octopus

Red abalone

Thresher shark

Rock crab

Bat ray

Bat star

Purple-striped
jelly

Brown pelican

Kelp

For All Sea Searchers

Sea searchers live all over the world. But whether up in
the mountains, out in a desert or near the seashore,
all sea searchers share a love for the sea and have an interest
to learn more about it. Sea searchers are curious. They
wonder about things, ask questions and figure out puzzling
problems. For some, being a sea searcher also means finding
ways to care for the sea—and finding ways to help others do
the same. Whatever you choose as a sea searcher, remember
you're a steward of the sea; one who knows, loves and cares
for the sea and, ultimately, makes wise decisions respectful
of planet Earth.

To All Sea Searcher Guides

In this book, you'll discover a treasure
of activities, from art to science, and from
math to language arts. Such a variety allows
people of all kinds and all ages to explore and
discover the wonders of the sea.

SEARCHING SEA HABITATS

SEARCHING SEA HABITATS

A Habitat Is Home

Homes in the Sea

The sea is one of the richest, most diverse areas in the world: rich because it supports an amazing number of plants and animals, diverse because its varied features form a wide array of habitats, or homes. From the two-mile-deep submarine canyon to the wave-swept rocky shore, each habitat is unique. And as you explore them, you'll make a discovery: each habitat has its own special character, living conditions and associated community of plants and animals specially adapted to life there.

In every habitat, plants and animals face the same challenges: they must find food, defend themselves and their homes and live long enough to reproduce—all of these in order to survive as a species. When you investigate the sea's plants and animals, whether at home, at school, along the shore or at an aquarium, you can discover even more about each plant and animal by thinking about its habitat and how well it's suited for life.

The rocky shore

Life is hard between the tide marks on the rocky shore. Crashing waves, drying sun and changing tides set the conditions for life along the shores; here, as on the wharf pilings, plants and animals

Brittle star

aren't randomly distributed but occur in bands or zones.

The high-tide zone is more land than sea; only a few specially adapted plants and animals can survive. The plants and animals that live here receive most of their moisture through wave splash. To avoid drying out, barnacles close their shells and limpets go out only at night.

In the mid-tide zone lives a diverse group of animals and plants, including seaweeds, mussels and sea stars. Community members must find ways to stay moist when the tide is out, avoid predators when the tide is in and compete with each other for space.

The low-tide zone is exposed to air only during the lowest of low tides. As they're usually covered by water, the residents are subject to sea stars, fishes and other predators that range into shallow waters.

The sandy shore

Like the sandy seafloor, a sandy shore seems barren. But where straggly dune plants take root, they build and stabilize the dunes, creating places where others can grow.

On "empty" sandy beaches, shorebirds like sandpipers and godwits forage, finding food at the water's edge, in the tidal debris and on the higher, drier beach. Meanwhile, the beach dwellers—permanent residents like Pismo clams, beach hoppers and sand crabs—burrow into the sand for protection from such predators. Beach animals also face waves and changing tides; those that can't dig back down fast need to keep moving on.

Pismo clam

The wetlands

From saltmarshes and tidal creeks to mud flats and sloughs, wetlands represent a variety of habitats, each with its own set of conditions and community of life.

The saltmarsh is a highly productive plant community that also provides nesting and resting space for shorebirds. Plants like pickleweed and eelgrass live in zones set by their ability to tolerate the salty soil and compete with other plants. Since few creatures can take the stressful conditions (extreme variations in temperature and salinity), there aren't many different kinds of them in a saltmarsh. But creatures that are here are present in great

Pipefish with eelgrass

numbers, because of the food produced by pickleweed.

Tidal creeks bring seawater into the salt-marsh and provide habitat for many fishes and invertebrates. They also act as nurseries for young fishes like bat rays, leopard sharks, surfperches and flatfishes. Some move on to the sea, but some stay here all their lives.

Little life is apparent on a mud flat; most animals here burrow for cover. Worms and clams are among the best-suited mud dwellers; their burrows or siphons connect them with food and oxygen above. At low tide, shorebirds poke around for food and harbor seals haul out on the flats to bask.

The kelp forest

Giant kelp plants form vast, underwater forests close to the shore in certain parts of the world. These complex natural communities provide food and shelter for a great variety of plants and animals. Within the kelp forest habitat are many microhabitats, from the tangled rootlike holdfast on the seafloor hiding brittle stars and crabs to the canopy of fronds reaching 20 to 100 feet above (6 to 30.5 meters), sheltering fishes and other creatures.

Some fishes, like blue rockfish, swim in the open water between kelp plants, while others, like giant kelpfish, hover near kelp blades, mimicking their color and shape.

Blue rockfish

In dark places where light-loving seaweeds can't grow, attached animals like sponges and anemones thrive. A turf of attached animals and plants carpets rock faces, offering cover for small fishes and invertebrates.

The open sea

The open sea is a world without walls. It's a place where there's nothing to cling to and nowhere to hide. Currents set the tempo for life, pushing along the plankton: tiny drifting plants and animals that feed all the ocean's creatures. Their transparent bodies help plankton hide in the open, while spines and oil droplets slow their sinking.

The larger, free-swimming animals (called nekton) have different adaptations, often involving camouflage, buoyancy and speed. Nekton include animals like seals, whales and fishes. Most open-water fishes are strong, streamlined swimmers; a number of them stay in schools. Blue sharks, salmon and mackerel glide smoothly through the open water. Many such fishes are countershaded

(dark backs and light undersides), a common camouflage technique here.

The deep sea

The cold, dark, constant waters of the deep sea shelter a community of little-known animals, often bizarre. Many, like the lanternfish, produce their own light (bioluminescence). Others, like the viperfish, have small bodies and huge fangs. Below 600 feet (183 meters), there's no sunlight; because no plants survive, the animals prey on each other, migrate at night to find food near the surface or feed on organic matter that falls from above (marine snow).

Scientists are studying the deep sea habitat off the Atlantic coast, off the coast of Japan and in Monterey Canyon (just offshore in Monterey Bay, California). The Monterey Canyon is

Blue shark

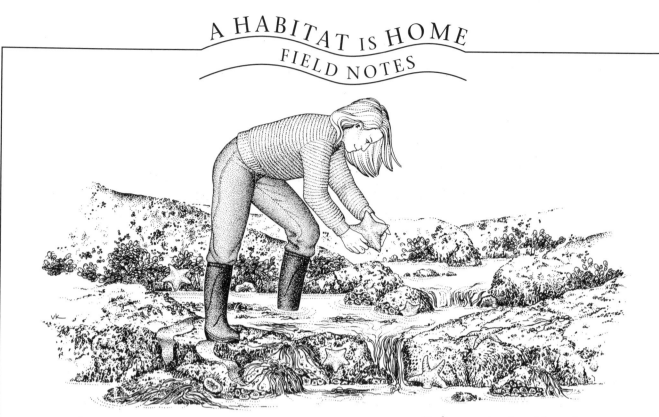

Finding sea stars in a tide pool

about twice as deep and one-third the length of the Grand Canyon. This huge chasm cuts the bay nearly in half, sloping down from a depth of about 60 feet (18 meters) at Moss Landing to nearly 12,000 feet (3,656 meters) at its end 60 miles (97 kilometers) out to sea.

Blue shark tail

Ocean habitats and people

Since the days of coastal Indians, people have used the oceans in many ways, from fishing and hunting to travel and recreation. Some habitats, like the rocky shore, are so accessible to us their balance can easily be destroyed; others, like the submarine canyon, have only just begun to be explored.

Sandy shore beaches are popular sites for home building and recreation. And because they're so accessible, rocky shores are one of the best-known, most-studied habitats anywhere. Lessons biologists learn in tide pools translate into knowledge about living systems all over the world.

Wetlands provide a valuable habitat for wildlife, and they're havens to bird watchers, clam diggers, nature lovers and sport fishermen.

Besides our growing use of products that contain kelp extracts (algin is used in toothpaste, ice cream and paint), kelp forests attract thousands of divers and sport fishermen each year. They're also the focus of bird- and otter-watchers, who enjoy their sport from shore.

What's Your Favorite?

MATERIALS
- Paper
- Pen or pencil
- Your favorite drawing materials

Memories of favorite experiences are an important part of life. They're what make your life special for you. Think about your favorite ocean experience or animal. Write a story or draw a picture about it. Why is it your favorite? Do you remember any smells or sounds? Was anyone else with you? If you'd like, share your story or picture with someone else.

Home Sweet Home

MATERIALS
- Several sheets of drawing paper
- Your favorite drawing materials
- A shoe box or food carton for the base of a model
- Arts and crafts materials for your model

What makes a home a home? Draw a picture or build a model of your own home. What kind of environment is your home in? (Is it near the ocean, in a desert, in a forest?) What is your house made from? What kinds of things do you have in your room that make it special? Where do you get your food? If you could rebuild your house, how would you design it? How could you build it to have the least amount of impact on the environment as possible? What other things do you need to live?

Now draw an ocean animal in its home; for instance, a sea otter in a kelp forest. How does the life of this animal differ from your life? How are your lives the same? What does your animal eat and where does it get its food? What kind of shelter does it need in order to survive? What body parts help provide shelter? How does it move? How does it protect itself?

Every Home Is Different

A coyote lives in the uplands.

A great blue heron visits a saltmarsh.

MATERIALS
- Field Guide pictures from various chapters in this book
- Large sheet of paper for a collage or mural
- Magazines
- Your favorite drawing materials

an animal that lives in the kelp forest live at the rocky shore? Could it live in the deep sea? Why or why not? Using the Field Guides, pictures from magazines or ones you draw, make a collage or mural of your favorite ocean habitat.

Some people live in cottages by the sea, others live on ranches in the valleys of rolling hills. Just as people live in different kinds of homes, animals live in different kinds of homes, too. A sea otter swims through a lush kelp forest, a sand dollar rests on the sandy seafloor and a lanternfish blinks lights in the dark deep sea. After collecting pictures from the Field Guides, sort them according to habitat. Could

California halibut

The Ocean Planet

MATERIALS
- An apple
- A knife

Did you know that of all the water on the planet, 97 percent is in the oceans and only about three percent is available as fresh water to drink? And of that three percent, did you know that most of it is in the form of ice in polar or mountain glaciers? This means only one percent of the Earth's water is available as fresh water. To compare these amounts, cut an apple into quarters. Take one quarter (25 percent) and cut it in half to represent 12 percent. Now take one of those halves and cut it in half to show six percent. Cut one of those halves in half again to show three percent. This one slice represents all of the fresh water in the world, while the rest of the apple represents the oceans. The water we have today is the only water we'll ever have on this planet. As a matter of fact, the water we drink today is the same water a dinosaur may have drunk millions of years ago, or the water Christopher Columbus used for brushing his teeth. We must keep today's water clean . . . it's the only water we have for tomorrow.

Within the world's oceans are many different kinds of habitats: the kelp forest, coral reefs and rocky shores are a few. Research an ocean habitat you've visited or would like to visit, noting its special conditions and the plants and animals that live there. For instance, at the sandy beach you find shifting sand, crashing waves and changing tides; clams, shorebirds and drift kelp. In the deep sea you find darkness, cold water and high pressure; anglerfish, lanternfish and deep sea squid.)

Design an Underwater World

Design an underwater world that people could live in, then draw or build a model of it. What are some of the problems in transferring a land-based community to the sea? What kinds of materials would you use for the buildings? How would people breathe? Where would they get food and fresh water? How would they communicate? How would they dispose of waste? Do you think people should build and live in underwater cities? How would these cities affect the sea's plants and animals?

MATERIALS
- Paper and pencil or other favorite drawing materials
- A shoe box, food carton or other material for the base of your model
- Arts and crafts materials for your model and to make ocean plants and animals

MAKE YOUR MODEL WITH DOUGH

You'll need:

1 cup salt

1 cup flour

1/2 cup water

Bowl

Paints and paint brush

Mix together the salt, flour and water to make a dough. Then form the dough into a model of your underwater world. Paint your world, then use a variety of arts and crafts materials to create plants and animals for their ocean home.

It's Show Time!

MATERIALS
- Paper
- Pen or pencil
- A variety of arts and crafts materials

Work with friends or classmates to write and perform your own play or puppet show about ocean habitats and the plants and animals that live there. Use arts and crafts materials to create props, puppets and backdrops. There are patterns and directions in this book to make a Clancy Clam Costume (pages 37–39), a Jelly Dress-Up (page 81), a Snazzy Squid Suit (pages 83–85) and an Ollie Otter Puppet (pages 138–139). Invite your friends, family and neighbors to enjoy the show.

SEARCHING SEA HABITATS

The Rocky Shore

What Is the Rocky Shore?

The rocky seashore is an ideal place to investigate the mysteries of the sea. The regular rise and fall of sea level we call the tides has created one of the richest, most variable environments in the ocean. The narrow fringe of land and sea between the lowest and highest tidemarks is called the intertidal. During low tide, you can explore the seafloor; no other marine habitat is as accessible. Because of this, the rocky intertidal is the most thoroughly studied, best-known ocean area.

Wave force

Waves batter the rocky intertidal. During storms, a wave can hit the shore with the force of a car going 90 miles per hour. To protect themselves from being smashed by waves or torn from rocks, plants and animals here hold on, lie flat, bend with the waves or hide.

Many intertidal animals hold on tight to avoid being swept away. Snails and chitons have a strong, muscular foot. Sea stars have thousands of tiny tube feet with suction-cup ends. Mussels anchor themselves by gluing threads to the rocks; seaweeds have strong, rootlike holdfasts that cling to the rocks.

Lined shore crab

Body shape and structure help plants and animals survive crashing waves. The Chinese-hat shape of limpets and barnacles and the flat shape of chitons and abalone offer little resistance to the water rushing past. Snails, crabs, barnacles and mussels have strong shells to protect them. Flexible anemones bend rather than break; seaweeds, too, are smooth, strong and flexible.

Many animals escape the waves by hiding under plants, among other animals or between and under rocks. Crabs crawl into rock crevices and small, delicate animals like brittle stars hide under rocks or in mussel beds and kelp holdfasts.

Air exposure

Air exposure also creates problems for intertidal creatures. Falling tides expose them to highly variable air temperatures: sometimes hot, sometimes bitter cold.

Plants and animals left out of water must find ways to keep from drying out. To cope, some snails draw into their shells and seal them with doorlike operculums; some also secrete a mucous seal. Mussels close their shells tightly to retain water, and anemones gather in

California mussels

Tidepool sculpin

masses so that less body surface is exposed to the air. Many animals hide under rocks or seaweeds to avoid drying out.

Seaweeds are layered on rocks with upper layers shielding the lower layers so only a few plants are exposed. Some seaweeds can dry out completely, rehydrating when the tide returns.

At low tide, creatures submerged in tide pools may face low oxygen levels and widely fluctuating salinity. On warm days, evaporation raises salt concentrations; on rainy days, salt concentrations are lowered.

Competition and defense

To survive in the crowded intertidal, plants and animals must compete for space. Animals also need strategies to avoid being eaten. While the armorlike shells of crabs, barnacles and snails help protect them from predators, sea urchins and some intertidal fishes have spines. Other animals here are camouflaged like rocks and seaweeds; they're practically invisible. The tidepool

sculpin and octopus can change color and pattern to match their surroundings. And the decorator crab plants a garden of seaweeds, sponges and other sessile (attached) creatures on its back to escape detection. The same refuges that help protect an animal from the waves also protect it from predators.

People and the rocky shore

Intertidal creatures can survive harsh conditions, but not human carelessness. In the past, people collected animals by the bucketful. Now, strict laws govern the collecting of plants and animals in the intertidal. If you visit, do your part to preserve the community: turn each rock back, and leave everything as you find it.

Red octopus

Zonation

The intertidal can be divided into horizontal bands based on the length of time each is exposed to the air.

The **spray zone** is out of the water almost all the time, covered completely only during the highest of high tides. Few plants and animals can survive such harsh conditions. The plants and animals that do live here need the saltwater spray that wets this zone, but most of them couldn't survive long being submerged.

The **high-tide zone** is out of the water most of the time and completely covered only during high tides. Creatures here also tolerate long air exposure. Some of them would prefer living the lower-stress life in the lower intertidal, but they'd either get eaten or couldn't compete for space.

The **mid-tide zone** is usually covered and uncovered twice each day. The great variety of plants and animals living here spend more time under water than exposed.

The **low-tide zone** is exposed to the air only for a few hours each month during minus tides. Many plants and animals can't live in a higher tide zone because they can't tolerate much exposure.

The Tides of History

Tides, the regular rise and fall of the water along the ocean's shores, have intrigued people for a long time. Early Greeks noticed that the tidal cycle was tied to the phases of the moon. However, it wasn't until 1687, when Isaac Newton stated the laws of gravity, that a cause was discovered for this effect: the moon's gravity reaches out and pulls the ocean's water toward itself.

Figure 2

Forces creating the tides

Three major forces shape the tides. The moon pulls out a tidal bulge of water on the moonward side of the Earth. On the other side of the Earth, an equal and opposite bulge is created as the moon's gravity is less on the water than it is on the Earth (Figure 1). The sun's gravity also affects the tides, but because the sun is so far away, it pulls with only about half the moon's force.

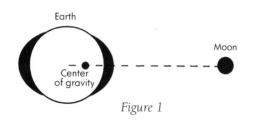

Figure 1

The two bulges on opposite sides of the Earth are like two giant waves of water that travel across our seas. The bulges cause the world's high tides; the low-water troughs between them cause low tides. A viewer in space would notice that the bulges remain fixed in their relationship to the moon, but the Earth rotates beneath them. Because the Earth moves relative to the bulges of water, those of us on dry land see the high water come and go as tides.

Tidal patterns

A given point on the Earth rotates beneath two tidal bulges each day. In theory, this causes two high and two low tides each day, but things aren't really so simple. As the Earth rotates, the moon is also traveling in its 28-day orbit of the Earth (Figure 2). Each day the Earth's rotation lags behind the moon's by about 50 minutes. For this reason, both moonrise and the tidal cycle start 50 minutes later each day. Tides cycle in a lunar day instead of our familiar solar day.

Tides vary in their height from day to day, due in part to the sun's influence (Figure 3). When the sun and moon line up (during a full or new moon) their gravitational pulls combine. This

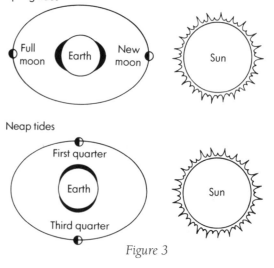

Figure 3

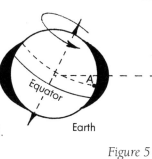

Figure 5

creates extreme high and low tides called spring tides (as in water that "springs up").

(call it Monterey) will pass beneath the deepest part of the first tidal bulge, but just catch the edge of the second one.

When the sun and moon are at right angles to each other, during first and third quarters of the moon, their pulls tend to cancel each other. This produces neap tides, where the range between high and low tides is the slightest.

In all, about 400 different factors combine to determine our tides. Local tide tables, available in bait shops and marine supply stores, use all these factors to predict tidal times and heights.

Marine life and the tides

Marine plants and animals that live close to the intertidal shore must cope as the tide comes and goes. Some species can stand exposure to air better than others; they commonly live higher along the shore than do more sensitive species. Such distribution patterns have led biologists to break the intertidal into zones, with predictable types of plants and animals living in each. Local biologist Ed Ricketts ("Doc" of John Steinbeck's *Cannery Row*) proposed such a system for this coast in his 1939 book, *Between Pacific Tides*. He called the highest, driest zone, which is wetted only by sea spray and occasional wave splash, Zone I. Tides regularly cover and uncover Zones II and III, while Zone IV is exposed to the air only during the lowest of tides.

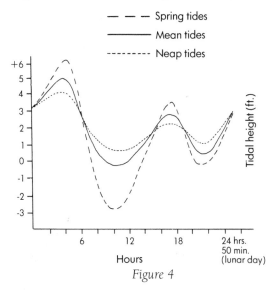

Figure 4

Tidal patterns also depend on where you are in the world. On North America's eastern coast, the tide ebbs and flows only once a day. Along the western coast there are two tides daily, one more extreme than the other—a "mixed semi-diurnal" pattern. Another orbital oddity accounts for this pattern: the moon doesn't circle directly above our equator.

The illustration (Figure 5) shows how this affects our tides. In the course of the day shown, Point A

The ability of a plant or animal to withstand the force of crashing waves or avoid predators also plays a part in where it settles. But the ebb and flow of the tides, more than anything else, sets the pattern of life along our coast.

A Trip to the Sea

Make a journal with drawings and words.

When the tide turns

Count the number of seconds between waves. Does the number change? Count seven waves, then put a stick in the sand to mark the wave's furthest point. Play for awhile at the beach, then return later to see where your stick is. Is it under water? Do the waves reach it? What happened?

If you're planning a trip to the sea, make a rocky shore journal to bring with you. Before you go, record with words and drawings what you expect to find at the seashore and what you'd like to see while you're there. Then when you're at the seashore, record what you do find. How do your lists compare?

Hold on tight!

At the seashore, find an animal where the waves splash. Did you get splashed? Watch the animal closely. How does it hold on when the waves crash on it? How do other tide pool animals hold on?

Bat star

YOUR TRIP TO THE SEASHORE is a visit to the home of many, many plants and animals. Treat them gently, with kindness and respect; and leave them in their homes as you find them.

Living with the Tides

> **MATERIALS**
> • Papier-mâché and chicken wire or large chunks of foam
> • Paint and paint brushes
> • Pictures or drawings of tide pool plants and animals

Turn one corner of your room into a tide pool (or you can use a large cardboard box, if you'd like). Build rocks out of papier-mâché or foam and paint them. (Or you can make rocks from pillows, rolled-up towels and small cardboard boxes.) Hang pictures of your favorite animals in the habitat. Then invite others to visit your tide pool. On the first visit, tell them they can collect animals; on the second visit, they can't. Compare how the tide pool looks each time. Which tide pool would you like to visit again? Why? What happens to your tide pool when you move rocks? What happens when you leave litter?

Sometimes Wet, Sometimes Hot

> **MATERIALS**
> • Tide table (from a local bait shop, sporting goods store or dive shop)
> • Several sheets of graph paper
> • Pencil

Learn to read the tide table by using the directions in the table. Graph the tides (horizontal X-axis = time of day, vertical Y-axis = height of tide) for either a week or a month. On each sheet of paper, graph a different day.

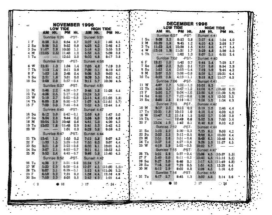

Now check your tide table or look in your newspaper to see the different moon phases. Record on each graph the moon's phase for that day. Tape the graphs together around the wall of your room for a continuous record. How does the moon's phase relate to the tide? What is the best time and date to go tide pooling?

At low tide, animals are exposed to the drying air and warming sun.

Drying Out

Across the top, make two columns: your guess and what actually happens.

Now leave your pieces for one hour, six hours and one day. Compare the different pieces to the shapes of tide pool animals. Are any of your pieces similar to the way an animal finds cover at the seashore? Which of your towel pieces is like a seaweed? Which one is like a barnacle, a sea star, a mussel? How do these animals keep from drying out during low tide?

Tear each sheet of paper towel into four pieces. Using the crayon or pencil, give each piece a different number or letter. Now experiment with folding the pieces into different sizes and dipping them in the fresh or salt water. Wad up some pieces into tight balls, fold some once, fold some a few times and fold some not at all. Dip some in the fresh water and some in the salt water. Place some in the plastic bags and leave some exposed to the air. Leave some in a sunny spot and some in the shade. Now, take a guess . . . what do you think will happen? Which ones will dry the fastest? Which will dry the slowest? Make a chart to record your experiments. Going down the left side of your paper, list what you did to the paper towel.

MATERIALS
- One cup of fresh water
- One cup of salt water (one tablespoon of salt in one cup of water)
- Several sheets of paper towels
- Two or three sandwich-size plastic bags
- Crayon or pencil

Once Upon a Time...
It was a dark
and windy night...

Pick a rocky shore animal and write a story about its life from the animal's point of view. What happens when a wave comes crashing in? How does it protect itself from waves? How does it keep from drying out? How does it find and catch food? What happens when a predator approaches? Who does it meet when the tide is high? Who does it meet during low tide?

MATERIALS
- Paper
- Pen or pencil

What Do You Think?

MATERIALS
• Paper
• Pen or pencil

Make a list of the different ways people use the shore. Place a (-) by the uses you feel have a negative effect on shoreline communities and a (+) by those you feel have a positive effect. Compare your results. How could negative effects be eliminated? What can you do to help eliminate them?

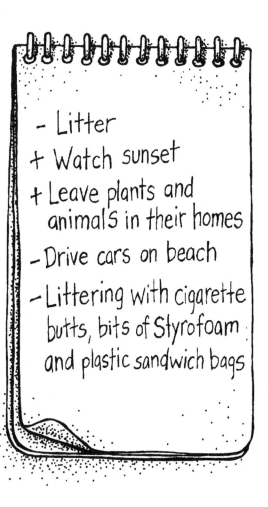

- Litter
+ Watch sunset
+ Leave plants and animals in their homes
- Drive cars on beach
- Littering with cigarette butts, bits of Styrofoam and plastic sandwich bags

News Bulletin

MATERIALS
• Bulletin board
• Current magazines and newspapers

Make a bulletin board titled "Shorelines in the News." Post current news articles on storms, fishing, sand castle contests, seaside development, oil spills, surfing and other events or issues.

Tide Pool Coloring Sheet

MATERIALS
• Your favorite coloring tools— markers, colored pencils, watercolors or crayons
• Pen or pencil

The following page is a coloring sheet. If you'd like, make copies of it first so you can color it many different times— and many different ways. Go nuts!

Tidepool sculpin

Oligocottus maculosus SIZE: TO 8 IN. (20 CM)

A tidepool sculpin is hard to see because its colors match the rocks and plants around it. A sculpin on sea lettuce won't look like one living on gray rocks. At high tide, this fish travels about looking for small animals to eat. At low tide, it hurries back to its tide pool. Even if it goes exploring nearby pools, a sculpin can find its way back home.

Ochre star

Pisaster ochraceus SIZE: TO 1 FT. (30 CM)

This sea star has hundreds of tiny suction-cup feet under each arm that help it stick to rocks. The sea star is a real loafer; it clings motionless on a rock for weeks. Even a hungry sea star isn't hasty. Slow and steady, its feet can pry apart a mussel. When the mussel's two shells open, the sea star slides its stomach between the shells to digest the animal inside.

Red octopus

Octopus rubescens size: to 20 in. (50 cm)

Like magic, this octopus can change its color and shape in a flash. It can also squeeze through small holes to hide in caves or under rocks. A hiding octopus keeps out of danger. And a quick armful of suckers can surprise a crab or fish. The octopus's body is soft except for a parrotlike beak that's sharp enough to kill and tear up food.

Sea lettuce

Ulva sp. SIZE: TO 8 IN. (20 CM)

Sea lettuce is as green as lettuce from land, but it's only two cell-layers thick. Although it's thin and fragile-looking, sea lettuce can survive pounding waves and drying sun These plants are weeds: they quickly overgrow bare rocks. Just as quickly, sea lettuce is gobbled up by snails and crabs.

Lined shore crab

Pachygrapsus crassipes SIZE: TO 2 IN. (5 CM)

The shore crab dances sideways down to the sea and then back up over the rocks. Using tiny cups on its pinchers, the crab scrapes small plants off the rock to eat. This crab is so flat, it can hide in cracks in the rocks. If a hungry gull grabs the shore crab's leg, the crab can shed the captured limb and dash away. In time, a new leg will grow back.

Sea slug

Hermissenda crassicornis SIZE: TO 3 IN. (8 CM)

This blue-and-orange sea slug is a cruel beauty. It tastes terrible and it has stingers. Maybe the bright colors warn other animals, "Don't mess with me!" This sea slug eats all kinds of animals, some small, some large, some already dead. When two hungry sea slugs meet, they may fight a terrible battle to the death.The loser becomes the breakfast of champions.

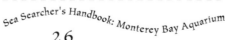

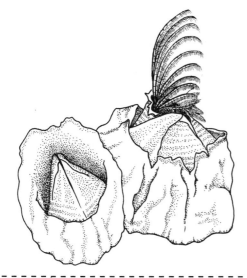

Barnacle

Balanus glandula SIZE: TO 1 IN. (2.5 CM)

A young barnacle cruises at sea during its first weeks free from mother. When it's ready to settle down, the barnacle glues its head to a rock and builds a shell. As sea water rushes by, the barnacle's legs kick bits of food down into its mouth. Its shell closes tight at low tide, so the barnacle stays moist. It makes a juicy meal for a shorebird with a prying beak.

Sea anemone

Anthopleura elegantissima SIZE: TO 10 IN. (25 CM)

The sea anemone looks like a flower on a thick, bumpy stalk, but it's really an animal. The flowery parts are tentacles with stingers. The stingers zap small animals that get too close; then the anemone swallows them whole. At low tide, the anemone closes up. Bits of shell stuck to the bumpy flesh help keep the sea anemone from drying out.

Brown turban snail

Tegula brunnea SIZE: TO 1 IN. (2.5 CM)

At low tide, the brown turban snail stays under water or low on the shore. A hungry snail scrapes algae with its filelike tongue, or radula. One lick from this snail can leave scrape marks on kelp. If a wave flips a snail upside-down, it can pick up pebbles with its foot. By rolling with the added weight, the snail can turn right side up again.

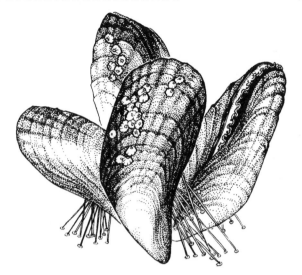

California mussel

Mytilus californianus SIZE: TO 5 IN. (13 CM)

Mussels crowd together on wave-swept rocks. To hang on to the rocks and each other, mussels make strong threads that look like plastic and stick better than super strong glue. A mussel eats by filtering tiny plants and animals from the water. To collect enough food to survive, a mussel has to filter two to three quarts of water an hour.

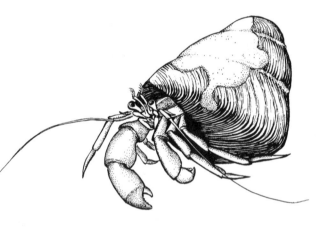

Hermit crab

Pagurus samuelis SIZE: TO 1 IN. (2.5 CM)

A hermit crab wears an empty snail shell to protect its soft body. The back legs hold the shell on tight. As the crab grows, it needs bigger shells. One hermit crab will even steal a good shell from another crab. Though a hermit crab threatens and fights with its large claws, it's not a hunter. This crab eats seaweeds and dead animals.

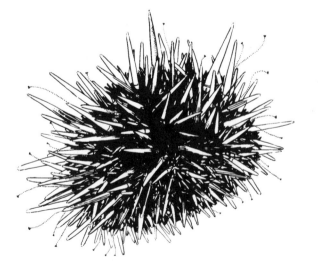

Purple sea urchin

Strongylocentrotus purpuratus

SIZE: TO 4 IN. (10 CM)

Using their spines and teeth, urchins burrow slowly into solid rock. Because they grow as they dig, some end up trapped in holes, too big to leave. Between the hard spines, an urchin has hundreds of tube feet. Its soft tube feet are always busy: some hold the urchin onto the rock; others move kelp to the urchin's greedy mouth.

SEARCHING
SEA
HABITATS

The
Sandy Shore

What Is a Sandy Shore?

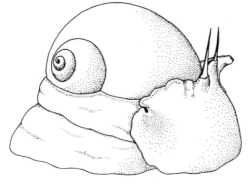

Moon snail

In many areas, the shore is surrounded by an almost continuous stretch of sandy beach, popular with swimmers, surfers, fishermen, beachcombers, bird watchers and clammers. But when the people are gone, the beach seems deserted—barren except for shorebirds and kelp flies. If you were to look closer, though, you'd see sandy shores that are filled with life: most of the inhabitants are in hiding. Many burrow into the sand for protection; there are even microscopic animals living between the grains.

Conditions are harsh

Wave action is one of the most important factors governing life on a sandy beach. Successive waves, changing tides and passing seasons continually restructure the beach. In winter, strong waves create steep-sloped beaches of coarse sand; in summer, gentle waves produce broad, flat areas of fine sand.

Sand protects burrowing animals. It hides them from the drying sun at low tide and buffers them from extremes in temperature and salinity.

How animals cope

Shifting sand offers no firm places to attach, so large marine plants and sessile (attached) animals cannot live here. The only large plants are beach-cast seaweeds. Large sandy beach animals are either visitors (birds and fishes) or burrowers, able to dig back down whenever waves uncover them. Polychaete worms, small clams and crustaceans are rapid diggers; pismo clams have heavy shells to anchor them. Burrowing protects sandy shore animals from predators as well as waves and drying sun.

Since no large plants live here, shore animals eat other animals or whatever food the water carries in. Most either scavenge dead plants and animals, filter tiny plant and animal plankton from the water (suspension-feeding) or eat debris from the sand (deposit-feeding).

Polychaete worm

Zonation

Animals live in different zones of the beach depending on their ability to withstand crashing waves and air exposure. These zones move up and down the beach with the tides.

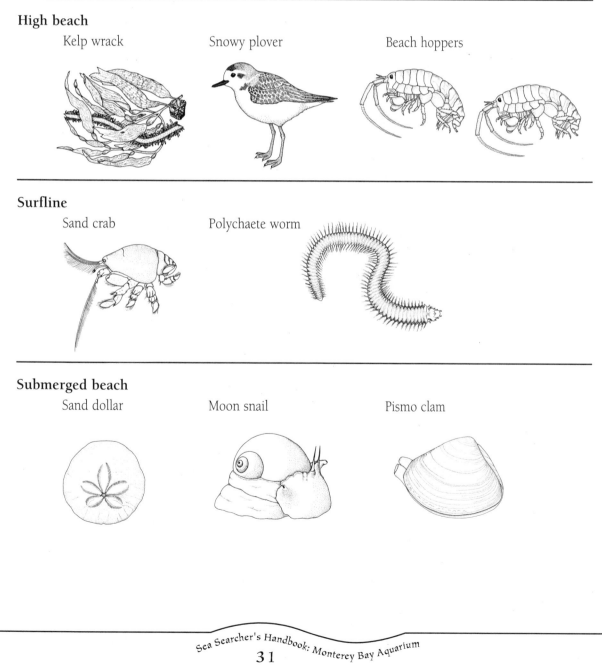

High beach

Kelp wrack   Snowy plover   Beach hoppers

Surfline

Sand crab   Polychaete worm

Submerged beach

Sand dollar   Moon snail   Pismo clam

Life between the tides

Though sandy shores support relatively few species, those that live here generally occur in great numbers. While different animals are found in different zones, many move up and down the beach with the tides. Because of this, zonation patterns along sandy shores are not as clearly defined as on rocky shores.

The higher part of the shore receives only the occasional wave, one which has spent most of its force on the lower beach. Piles of drift seaweed (wrack) are left high on the beach by the falling tides. Amphipods called beach hoppers burrow in moist sand where they're protected from shorebirds and waves. They stay in their burrows during the day, venturing out at night to feed on decaying animals and seaweed in the wrack. Beach isopods (which are related to pill bugs) are found a little farther down the beach, but still above the washing waves. Like amphipods, the isopods feed on wrack and detritus.

Sea lettuce

The mid-tide zone has periods of calm and periods of disturbance from wave action. The sand crab, a relative of the hermit crab, migrates up and down the beach to stay in the right spot to feed. Burrowing just beneath the surface, the sand crab faces up the beach, extending feathery antennae into the water to trap plankton and detritus from the wave wash. When a strong wave exposes it, the crab will quickly rebury itself. Polychaete worms, amphipods and mysid shrimps also live safely beneath the shifting layer of the sand here.

At the low-tide level the sand is kept in almost constant turmoil by the waves; this zone is rarely exposed to air. Though sand dollars usually live in subtidal areas beyond the surf, some live at low-tide levels. When wave surge threatens to dislodge them, they bury themselves completely. Young sand dollars store a few heavy sand grains in the gut for added weight and stability.

There are different predators prowling the sandy shore at high tide than at low tide. At high tide, fishes prey on crustaceans and worms. Just behind the surfline, sanddabs and surfperches feed on invertebrates

Sand dollar

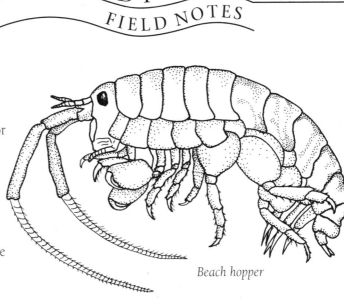

exposed by the waves. A major sandy shore predator, the moon snail, burrows along till it bumps into a clam. Using its radula (filelike tongue) to bore a hole in the clamshell, it eats the soft tissue inside.

Beach hopper

At low tide the sandy beach offers a feast of amphipods, wrack insects, worms and sand crabs for shorebirds like godwits, willets, turnstones and sanderlings.

People and beaches

Because of their beauty, beaches are popular for home building as well as recreation. But their summer serenity belies their changeable nature; it's the winter storms that smash houses that remind us how harsh a beach can be.

Though sandy beach creatures are well-adapted to survive the difficult conditions, they are vulnerable to human activity: house, jetty and pier construction, offroad vehicles and other recreational use. In some places clam digging has decimated extensive pismo clam beds (it's now strictly regulated). Many people who go to the beach never realize they're sharing this environment with an array of marine life. When you visit, walk with care. Remember its hidden secrets, and look for signs of life.

Snowy plover

Sandy Shore Survival Suit

MATERIALS

• A variety of clothes, scarves, fabrics and props to create a survival suit

Read about sandy shores on pages 30–33. What challenges do intertidal plants and animals face? (They face challenges like wave shock, air exposure and predation.) How do they cope? Design, draw and construct a shore-line survival suit that would make it possible to live between high and low tides. The suit should enable you to eat, protect yourself from crashing waves, hang on, stay under water part of the time, stay moist and meet the other challenges of life along the shore.

Crawl Like a Crab

MATERIALS

• Yourself!

Play a lively game of charades with your friends, family or classmates. Act out sandy shore animals, pantomiming how the animal gets its food, avoids predators, protects itself from waves, moves along the seafloor or swims through the water. Have others guess who you are.

A Sand Collection

MATERIALS

- Pencil and paper
- Containers with lids for your sand collection
- Magnifying lens
- Magnet
- Map of area from which you're collecting sand
- Glue

Create a sand collection for your room. Write to people that live along the shore in other states; ask them to describe their beaches, beach plants and animals and swap sand with samples with them. Compare the colors, smells, size of grains and how the sand feels when rubbed between your fingers. Take a close look at the grains with a magnifying lens. What effect does a magnet have on sand? Where do you think the different kinds of sand originated? Why are they different? Post a map and glue a sample of each kind of sand near its origin.

Make a Sandy Shores Book

Draw pictures of your home, including what you need to live (water, food, a safe place to sleep). What do sandy shore animals need to survive in their homes? Cut out magazine pictures and draw your own to make a book of you in your home compared to animals in their sandy shore home.

MATERIALS

- Paper
- Pen or pencil
- Your favorite drawing materials
- Magazines
- Scissors
- Glue

Seashore Math

MATERIALS
- Paper
- Pencil

Clam = 4 oz.
50 lb. otter

25% of 50 lbs. =
.25 X 50 = 12.5 lbs.
of food/day

12.5 lbs. X 16 oz. = 200 oz.
of food/day

$$\frac{200 \text{ oz.}}{4 \text{ oz.}} = 50 \text{ clams}$$

A 50 lb. otter eats
50 clams a day.

If you were a beach hopper, how far could you hop? Use the ratio: your height/x = length of hopper/distance hopper hops. For hopper length, use .8 inches (two centimeters) and for distance hopper hops, use 20 inches (50 centimeters).

A sea otter needs to eat approximately 25 percent of its body weight per day in food. If the meat in an average clam weighs four ounces (113 grams), how many clams would a 50-pound (23 kilograms) otter eat in one day?

It's Game Time!

MATERIALS
- Sandy Shore Field Guide (pages 40–43)
- Scissors

Game 1
Make two copies of the Sandy Shore Field Guide. Cut the pictures into individual cards and play "Concentration."

Game 2
Sort the pictures in the Sandy Shore Field Guide into different piles, then explain why you sorted them that way.

Game 3
Make several copies of the Sandy Shore Field Guide and use the cut-up cards to play "Go Fish."

Game 4
Secretly pick an animal from the Sandy Shore Field Guide. Have your partner ask "yes" and "no" questions to guess your animal.

MAKE UP YOUR OWN GAME
with the Sandy Shore Field Guide!

Get Involved!

What are some ways you can help protect shoreline communities? (Leave animals where you found them, pick up litter.) Why is it important to leave animals and shells where we find them?

Clancy Clam Costume

MATERIALS

- Foam (check the phone book for local foam or mattress stores)
- 6' x 7' sheet of 1" thick foam for shell, shell straps and foot band
- 6' to 9' of 1/2" thick foam for foot, gill band and siphons
- 12' of butcher paper or newsprint
- Contact cement or spray adhesive
- Scissors
- 2-1/2' of 3/4" Velcro
- 2 large costume feathers about 1' long
- Spray paint: 2 cans of beige and 1 can of a contrasting color like pink, yellow or brown
- 6" piece of electrical, packing or duct tape
- Highlighter pen
- Rubber gloves (optional)

To make Clancy Clam

Read all the directions and study the illustrations before constructing Clancy Clam. Find a comfortable, well-ventilated workplace and have clean-up materials handy. Read and follow the health warnings on the glue and paint containers.

1. Enlarge pattern pieces onto butcher paper or newsprint using an overhead projector. Outline the shell, foot, siphons, shell straps and gill and foot bands on the foam with a highlighter pen. Cut out the body parts.

2. Shell: Glue the two shell pieces together at the smallest ends (A), forming the hinge of the clam. (See illustration on page 39.) Glue the ends (B and C) of the straps vertically to the center of the shell. (You may want to wear gloves.)

3. Foot: Glue the foot (D) to its band (E), and glue Velcro to the ends (F and G).

4. Siphons: Glue the sides of the siphon pieces together to form two tubes (H). Glue the siphon tubes to the middle of the band (I), and glue Velcro to the ends (J and K).

5. Gills: Bind the shafts of the two feathers together with tape. Glue the joined feathers to the middle of the gill band at its lowest point (L), and glue Velcro to the ends (M and N).

Clancy Clam dress-up

Here's one way you can use the clam costume. If you're with a group, pick one volunteer to dress up as a clam. Discuss how the clam might be adapted to its living conditions, then show the clam's relevant body part. The dress-up might go something like this:

Shell: "Most clams live near the surf zone where waves crash. How could an animal with a soft body like this (point to volunteer) survive there?" (Wait for responses.) "Right, a hard shell protects the clam from being torn apart by waves or predators." (Have volunteer slip arms through the shell's straps, then close outstretched arms in front of body.)

Foot: "How do clams keep from being swept away by the waves?" (Wait for responses.) "A clam uses its strong foot to plow into the sand. Some bury themselves just below the surface, others can dig three feet or more down into the sand. The shell's heavy weight and streamlined shape help the clam burrow more easily."
(The foot goes inside the shell around the volunteer's waist and closes with Velcro.)

Siphons: "If a clam lives under the sand, how does it eat and breathe?" (Wait for responses.) "Clams have siphons like straws that they send up to the sand's surface. One siphon sucks in water, the other one pumps out waste. The incoming water contains oxygen to breathe and tiny plants and animals to eat. The deeper a clam lives in the sand, the longer its siphons must be to reach the water." (Siphons fit around volunteer's head and close with Velcro.)

Gills: "Clams also have gills to help them eat and breathe. Incoming water passes across the clam's gills. The gills absorb the water's oxygen (like a fish's gills) and trap small pieces of food." (Gills fit inside the shell around the student's neck with the feather pointing down and close with Velcro.)

Pismo clam

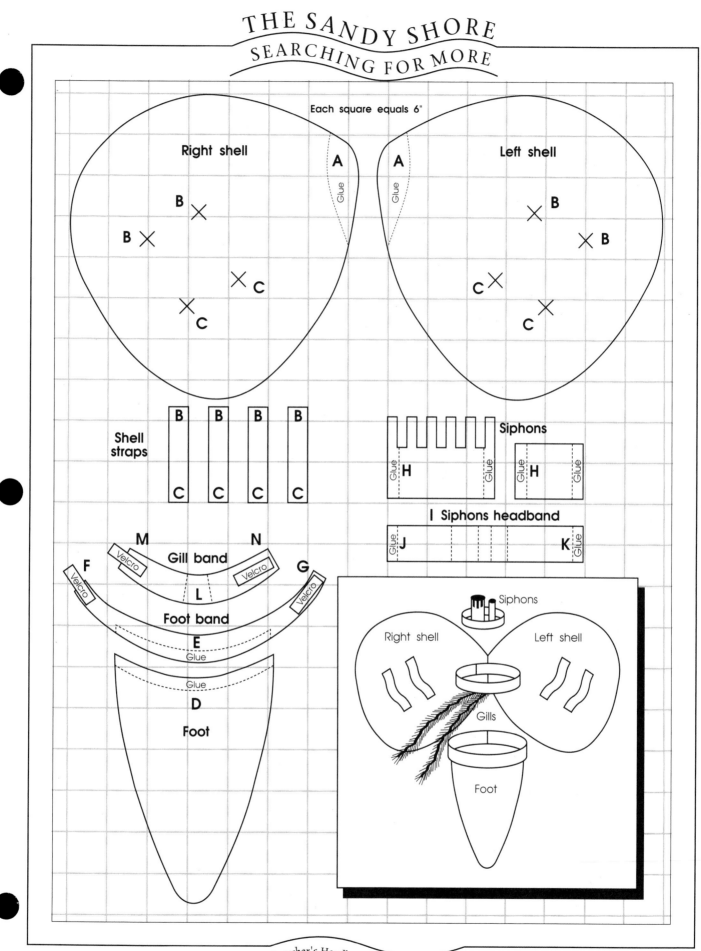

Each square equals 6"

Right shell

A Glue

Left shell

A Glue

B ✕

B ✕

C ✕

C ✕

B ✕

B ✕

C ✕

C ✕

Shell straps

B B B B

C C C C

Siphons

Glue H Glue

Glue H Glue

I Siphons headband

Glue J

K Glue

M Velcro

N Velcro

F Velcro

G Velcro

Gill band

L

Foot band

E

Glue

Glue

D

Foot

Siphons

Right shell

Left shell

Gills

Foot

Snowy plover

Charadrius alexandrinus SIZE: TO 6.5 IN. (16.5 CM)
Snowy plovers skitter about on the dry upper beach.
They hollow out their nests right on the sand. This is
safer than it might seem; both eggs and bird blend in
so well, they're almost impossible to see. Plovers eat
sand crabs, beach hoppers and other invertebrates.
They hunt in quick spurts, stopping to grab a bite,
then darting off again.

Sand crab

Emerita analoga SIZE: TO 1.4 IN. (3.5 CM)
Sand crabs live in the surf zone, following the tide
up and down the beach. To keep from washing
away, they burrow tail-first into the sand. Burrowing
also protects them from predators like surfperches
and plovers. To filter plankton from the water, a
sand crab sends fringed antennae up from the sand
into the passing waves.

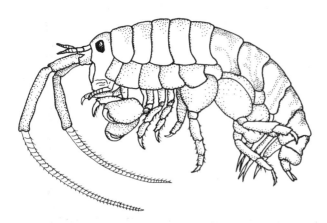

Beach hopper

Orchestoidea californiana SIZE: TO 1.1 IN. (2.8 CM)
Beach hoppers live high on the beach, out of reach
of the waves. They burrow during the day to keep
cool and moist and to hide from hungry
shorebirds. At night, they come out and hop about
in search of food. Beach hoppers eat the seaweed
that washes up on the beach.

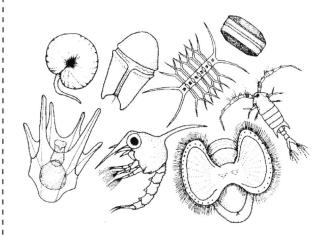

Plankton

(Plant plankton, top row from left: two dinoflagellates, chain diatom, diatom. Animal plankton, bottom row: sea urchin larva, crab larva, snail larva, copepod.) Plankton are plants and animals, mostly tiny, that drift on ocean currents instead of swimming. Plant plankton form the first link in many of the ocean's food chains. Animal plankton eat these tiny plants. Filter-feeders like clams and sand crabs eat both kinds of plankton.

Sand dollar

Dendraster excentricus SIZE: TO 3 IN. (7.6 CM) Sand dollars live half-buried in the sand just beyond the waves. They stand on end when the water is calm, but dig in during storms using their short spines. Young ones swallow heavy sand to weigh them down. Sand dollars feed on plankton and small organic particles found on the sand or in the water.

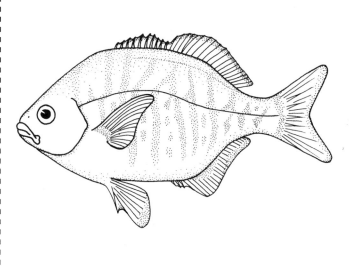

Barred surfperch

Amphistichus argenteus SIZE: TO 17 IN. (43 CM) Barred surfperch usually live in or just beyond the waves, but also venture into waters as deep as 240 feet (73 meters). Instead of releasing eggs, surfperches give birth to live young. Barred surfperch feed on sand crabs, clams and other invertebrates. Fishermen catch and eat surfperches, as do seals and larger fishes.

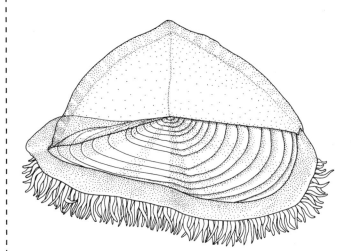

By-the-wind sailor

Velella velella SIZE: TO 3 IN. (7.6 CM)

By-the-wind sailors usually live far out to sea, but many get blown ashore in the spring. The angle of the sail may determine where they land. Those whose sails angle to the left are blown to our coast, while right-angled ones sail toward Japan. These jelly relatives use their tentacles to catch passing plankton.

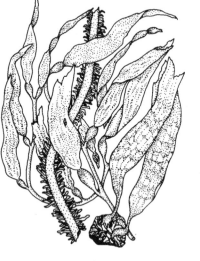

Drift seaweed

Rough waves rip seaweed from offshore rocks and toss it onto beaches. Often these tangles bring in offshore creatures that lived on the seaweed.These seaweeds are the only large plants you'll see on the beach, so they're centers of activity. Small animals like beach hoppers eat the decaying algae and hide beneath it. Larger animals like shorebirds come to hunt the small ones.

Pismo clam

Tivela stultorum SIZE: TO 6 IN. (15 CM)

Pismo clams dig into the sand near the surf zone. To dig, a clam pushes its foot downward through the sand like a wedge. Then it anchors the foot and pulls the shell along after it. A jet of water gives the shell an extra push from above. Clams send a feeding tube above the sand. They inhale water through it, filtering out tiny plants and animals called plankton.

Polychaete worm

Nephtys californiensis SIZE: TO 12 IN. (30 CM)
This sandworm is similar to earthworms, but
has a row of bristled flaps on each side. It burrows
through the beach sand. If a wave uncovers the
worm, it quickly swims down and digs in again.
This worm preys mostly on smaller sand-dwellers.

Moon snail

Polinices lewisii SIZE: TO 5 IN. (13 CM)
The moon snail plows slowly through the sand,
hunting for clams. Finding one, the snail surrounds
the shell with its huge foot. It drills a hole in the
shell, rasping with its filelike tongue and softening
the shell with a special liquid. When the hole is
finished, the snail eats the clam's soft insides.

Olive snail

Olivella biplicata SIZE: TO 1 IN. (2.5 CM)
The olive snail plows through the sand just below
the surface, leaving a furrow behind. Its smooth,
streamlined shell helps it slip through the sand. To
breathe, the snail sends a tube above the sand. The
olive snail eats dead animals and plants. It may also
gather tiny food bits from the sand.

SEARCHING SEA HABITATS

The Wetlands

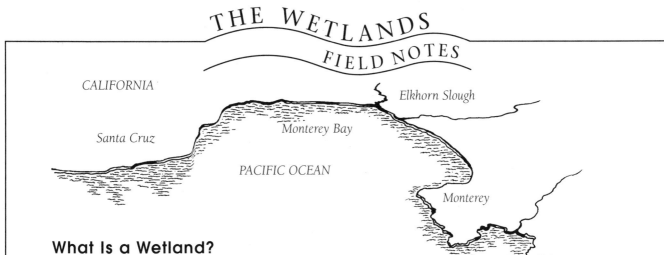

CALIFORNIA

Santa Cruz

Monterey Bay

Elkhorn Slough

PACIFIC OCEAN

Monterey

What Is a Wetland?

Water defines wetlands. And water controls the kinds of plants and animals that live there. The water may be salty or fresh, and a wetland may be always wet or sometimes dry. Wetlands, unlike rivers and lakes, are usually less than six feet (two meters) deep.

From swamps and bogs to marshes and sloughs, wetlands are found in every climate and region of the United States. Some are as small as a woodland pond covering less than an acre; others are as vast as Florida's Everglades, over a million acres in size.

A new look

In the past, most people considered wetlands as wastelands—places to be drained, plowed, filled and developed. And after the Swamp Land Act of 1849 made it legal to "reclaim" wetlands, millions of acres were destroyed.

Though this destruction has slowed, the country's remaining wetlands are still threatened by a growing human population. The need for more homes and more food means continued pressure to drain and destroy this habitat.

But today we have a better understanding of, and a new appreciation for wetlands. We now see them in their natural state as valuable wildlife habitat, fish nurseries, wintering grounds for migrating birds, water reservoirs and recreation areas. Wetlands filter and break down pollutants and control floods. And they provide jobs in fields like fisheries, wildlife and resource management, research and education.

Great blue heron

At the Edge of Monterey Bay

At the middle of the curve of Monterey Bay sits Elkhorn Slough (say "slew")—one of the largest remaining coastal wetlands in California.

Elkhorn Slough is considered a slough because it's a narrow, winding waterway edged with muddy and marshy ground. But Elkhorn Slough is also a seasonal estuary—a protected place where fresh water meets and mixes with sea water. After winter rains, fresh water runs off the surrounding land and mixes with the slough's salty water.

A diversity of life

Coastal wetlands support more life than most other ecosystems—and are more productive than most good farmlands. More than 80 species of fishes and 250 species of birds live in Elkhorn Slough during some part of their lives.

At Elkhorn Slough

One of the keys to this slough's great productivity is the abundance of tiny particles of decaying plants and animals, called detritus, floating in the water. Animals like fat innkeeper worms, bent-nosed clams and skeleton shrimp thrive on this rich fertilizer, supporting a food web of thousands of different kinds of animals. Some of the detritus comes from within the slough, primarily from

Bat ray

the marsh plants, and some of it is brought in from Monterey Bay with the tide.

Fishes come in from the ocean, too. Bat rays glide along just above the mud; their winglike fins stir up sediment to unearth clams and other burrowers. Leopard sharks, flatfishes, anchovies and sardines enter to feed on small fishes or plankton.

The mud flats

When the tide recedes, it exposes rich, dark mud. Seemingly lifeless at first glance, each cubic foot (.03 cubic meters) of mud may be crowded with thousands of crabs, shrimps, worms, snails, clams and other animals. The mud protects them from predators and the changes in both temperature and water conditions during daily tidal changes.

In spring and fall, the mud flats bustle with the comings and goings of thousands of migrating birds which stop here to rest, feed and breed. Curlews, godwits and willets probe the mud with their bills, hunting for burrowing crabs, worms and snails. Grebes and pelicans dive into the adjacent channel for small fishes, while mallards and other ducks dabble for algae.

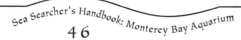

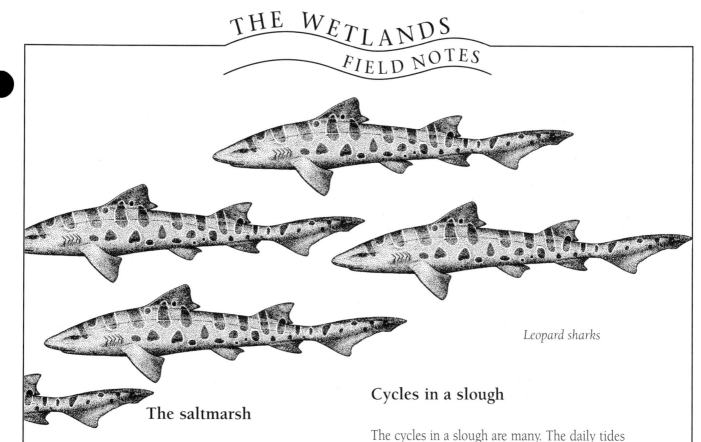

Leopard sharks

The saltmarsh

For a few days each month, when the moon is either in its full or new phase, the high tides top the mud flats, flooding the adjacent ground. This land is the saltmarsh: a habitat covered with low-growing, salt-tolerant plants.

While most plants would wither and die in these wet, salty conditions, pickleweed concentrates salt in the tips of its stems, then discards it when the tips drop off in the fall. Other plants like salt grass have special glands that secrete tiny cube-shaped crystals of salt.

The uplands

Further from the water, beyond the long stretches of saltmarsh, lie the uplands. Coast live oaks, coyote bush, sage and grasses grow on these drier hillsides, and spring carpets the hills with a colorful display of wildflowers. Hawks and golden eagles scan the uplands in search of rodents to eat.

Cycles in a slough

The cycles in a slough are many. The daily tides rise and fall, night becomes day and the seasons change. There are cycles of reproduction, migration, food webs, energy, water and nutrients. Each cycle affects the others in an ever-shifting balance of life and change. Together, along with the plants and animals, they create the complex ecosystem of the slough.

Changes over time

People, too, are part of a slough's ecosystem. At Elkhorn Slough for instance, Ohlone Indians began making their home there more than 4,000 years ago. Since then, our effect on Elkhorn Slough has progressed with the technological advances of humankind. In the 1700s, the Spanish grazed their cattle on the slough's native grasses. In the mid-1800s, Americans began logging and farming the uplands, causing erosion and introducing pesticides and non-native species: problems that continue to affect the slough today.

Brown pelicans

We now look at sloughs with a new perspective based on the lessons we've learned from the past. But their future depends on the decisions we make as voters and citizens. Today, part of Elkhorn Slough is a National Estuarine Research Reserve where research and education programs are conducted. And the waters of the Monterey Bay National Marine Sanctuary extend up the slough, increasing this wetland's protection. Together, these and other organizations hope to ensure the survival of this and other coastal environments—and to see that the cycles of life in them continue.

In the mid-1900s, engineers moved the slough's mouth. Originally, the slough's water flowed slowly behind the sandy beach and dunes north of Moss Landing before connecting with Monterey Bay. And sediment that washed down from local hillsides slowly filled the slough. But when engineers moved the mouth south to give boats direct access to Moss Landing's newly built harbor, they punched a permanent opening through the beach and dunes. This allowed water to flow in and out of the slough with greater force, scouring the channel's banks and, unfortunately, further eroding the saltmarsh and mud flat communities.

Skeleton shrimp

Songs about the Slough

Sing songs about the slough (pronounced "slew") . . . and make up your own verses!

"We're Going to the Slough"

Sung to the tune of *"The Farmer in the Dell"*

We're going to the slough,

We're going to the slough,

The slough's a type of habitat,

We're going to the slough.

We're passing pickleweed,

We're passing pickleweed,

Salty mud is where it lives,

We're passing pickleweed.

We're walking through the mud,

We're walking through the mud,

Keep your feet from getting stuck,

We're walking through the mud.

We're swimming in the water,

We're swimming in the water,

The water's cold and salty here,

We're swimming in the water.

A bat ray's swimming by,

A bat ray's swimming by,

Watch the bat ray slurp a clam,

A bat ray's swimming by.

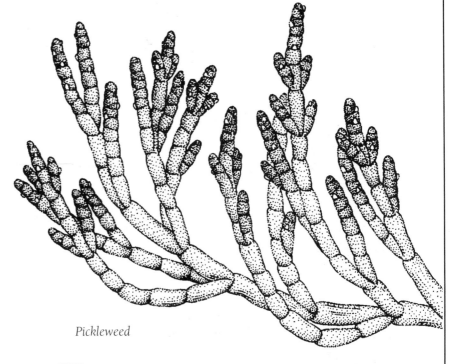

Pickleweed

"The Parts of the Slough"

Sung to the tune of "The Wheels on the Bus"

The mud in the slough goes squish, squish, squish,

Squish, squish, squish,

Squish, squish, squish,

The mud in the slough goes squish, squish, squish,

All day long.

The water in the slough is salty and cold,

Salty and cold,

Salty and cold,

The water in the slough is salty and cold,

All day long.

The tides in the slough move in and out,

In and out,

In and out,

The tides in the slough move in and out,

All day long.

The land near the slough goes from wet to dry,

Wet to dry,

Wet to dry,

The land near the slough goes from wet to dry,

All day long.

The animals in the slough they burrow and dig,

Burrow and dig,

Burrow and dig,

The animals in the slough they burrow and dig,

All day long.

The plants in the slough can be tiny or large,

Tiny or large,

Tiny or large,

The plants in the slough can be tiny or large,

All day long.

Pipefish in eelgrass

Look Who's in a Slough

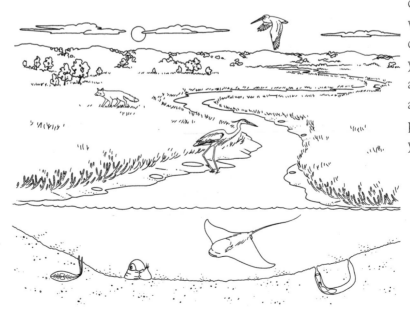

MATERIALS

- One copy each of pages 52 and 53. Enlarge images on a copier, if you'd like.
  - Crayons
  - Scissors
  - Paste
  - Pencils

Color the habitat scene, leaving the empty squares blank. The squares represent places where plants and animals can live in a slough. How many different habitats can you find at the slough? (Look for mud, water and land.) Cut up the small pictures into individual picture cards and sort them into groups. Why did you sort them the way you did? Color the picture cards, then fold each one in half along the dotted line. (The drawing will be hidden.)

Pick one picture square at a time and decide whether or not it belongs in a slough. If it does belong, paste the picture to the empty square that represents where it can be found in a slough. If you find things that don't belong, write the heading, "These don't belong in a slough" on the back of your habitat scene. Then paste the pictures of things that don't belong under that heading.

Which pictures did you put in your "These don't belong in a slough" pile? Do those things ever get into sloughs? How do they get there? Why don't they belong there? What happens to a slough's plants and animals when these things get into the slough? What would you do if you saw any of these things in a slough? Have you ever seen garbage in your backyard or school yard? What would you do about it?

Make a pledge. Some examples to get started are, "I will pick up trash when I see it and throw it away," or "I will recycle my trash whenever I can." Write your pledge on a piece of paper and put it in a place where you'll see it.

	Lined shore crab		Plankton
	Dog		Fat innkeeper worm
	Pickleweed		People
	Great blue heron		Bent-nosed clam
	Garbage		Boat
	Moon snail		Brown pelican

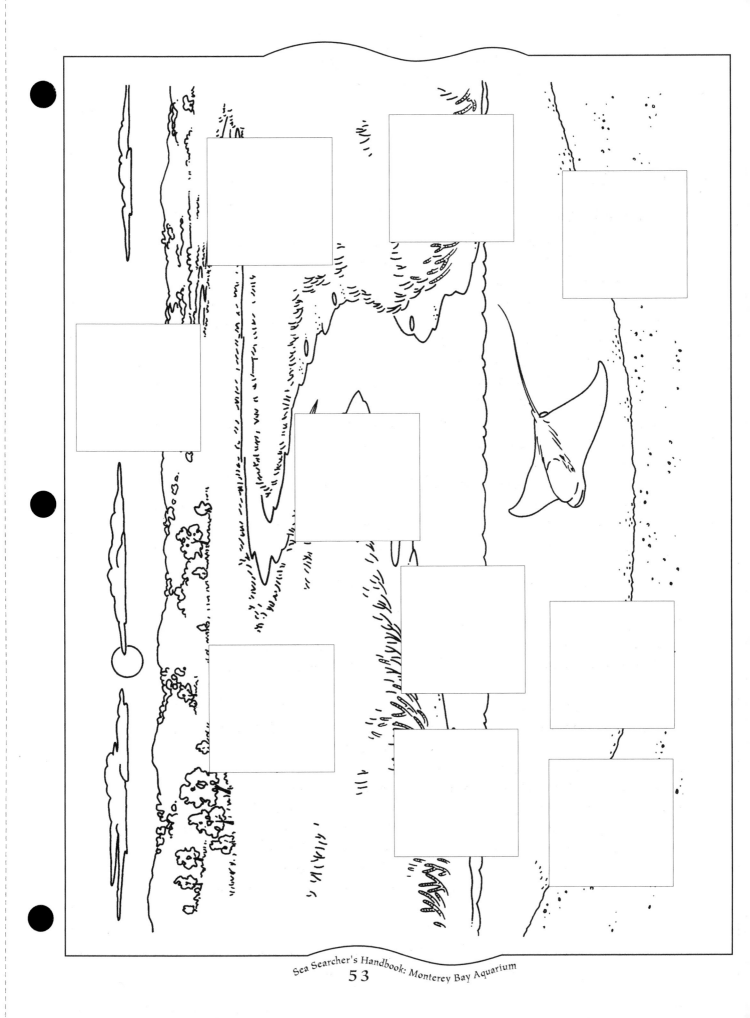

A Web of Life

MATERIALS
- Three copies of the front and back sides of the Wetlands Field Guide (pages 57–60)
- Scissors
- Masking tape
- Large ball of yarn or string
- Two blank pieces of paper, each cut in half to make four pieces total

An activity to do at school or at a party! You'll need at least 10 children.

Cut the Wetlands Field Guide into individual cards. You'll need one card for all but four children. On the blank sheets of paper, label one as sun, one as mud, one as water and one as air.

To begin, hand out one of the Wetlands Field Guide cards to all but four of the children. (If you're modifying this for a small class or party, be sure to use the plankton, bent-nosed clam, fat innkeeper worm, pickleweed, bat ray and great blue heron cards.) Hand out the sun, mud, water and air cards to the remaining four children.

Bent-nosed clam

Have children with identical cards get together into groups (for example, all the pickleweeds in one group, the moon snails in another). Have them read their cards and determine what their plants or animals eat and where they live. Have the sun, mud, water and air get together in one group to determine how they're necessary to the survival of slough plants and animals. (The sun provides energy which plants use to make food; mud provides a place for plants and animals to live; water provides transport; and air provides oxygen.) Have children tape the cards to their chests.

Come back together as a group. Ask children to define "interaction" and give some examples of different ways plants and animals interact with each other and with their habitat (for example, the relationship between an animal and the animal it eats, or the interactions between an animal and the temperature, currents and other characteristics of its home).

Outside, arrange the children in one large circle by groups so all the pickleweeds stand together, all the moon snails stand together and so on. The sun, mud, water and air should be interspersed among the other children in the circle. (Children can sit or stand for this.)

Have each group briefly report or act out (but not read) to the rest of the circle who they are, what they eat and where they live. Ask children if they think all of these living and non-living things could be connected to each other through their interactions.

Hand the ball of yarn to one child from one of the groups and ask that group to decide who or what their plant or animal interacts with. Then have him or her toss or roll the ball of yarn to one person in that group and explain how they interact with one another. For example, a bat ray might throw the yarn to a clam (what it eats) who might throw the yarn to the mud (where it lives).

Continue this until each child has gotten the yarn at least once. Ask children what they can tell you about the web. Point out (if they haven't already!) that everything in the slough is interconnected, then ask them if anything stands out as being more important than the others.

Read the following scenarios to the children, one at a time, and follow the directions in parentheses at the end of each one.

1. "People dig for clams and fat innkeeper worms to use as bait when fishing." (Have clams first, then fat innkeeper worms, gently tug on the yarn. Ask children to raise their hands when they feel the tugging and to tug on the yarn in return.)

2. "Gourmet food industry discovers pickleweed and starts harvesting it to make slough cookies." (Have pickleweeds tug on yarn and ask children to raise hands and tug back.)

3. "Eucalyptus trees are cut down because they're not native to the slough. This destroys the great blue heron nesting sites." (Have great blue herons tug on yarn and ask children to raise hands and tug back.)

4. "An office building is built on top of the mud." (Have all children gently pull on the yarn. Then you can either cut the yarn or ask all children to drop the yarn in front of them. If you cut the yarn, have children put the yarn down on the ground in front of them as they feel it go limp.)

5. "Local citizens write letters and attend public hearings to stop construction of the new office building on the mud flat." (Ask children to pick up yarn, then tie it back together if cut.)

What happened to the slough?

Animal Riddles

Sea hare

Here are a few for you to try, then make up your own.

I don't have a shell and I crawl across the mud looking for seaweed to eat. (sea hare)

I crawl in the mud and drill holes in the shells of my food. (moon snail)

I use my big fins that look like wings to swim over the mud. (bat ray)

I burrow in the mud and build a net to trap my food. (fat innkeeper worm)

Get Involved!

List some of the things your class or family can do to help protect wetlands and other threatened habitats in your area. Some ideas are: a family volunteers to help replant native plants, a student volunteers to assist a researcher who's studying shorebirds, a class raises money for a conservation project to restore a local habitat and two students visit a farm or industry and prepare a report on what these operations are doing to be good environmental neighbors.

A Wetlands Celebration

Plan an annual Habitat Protection Day or Habitat Protection Week for your community or school. Design ways to share why the habitat is important and how others can become involved in protecting and, if needed, restoring it. You might even want to set up field trips to your special habitat. School celebrations could be in conjunction with National Estuaries Day events happening locally as part of the annual Coastweeks celebration.

SAVE WETLANDS

Bat ray

Myliobatis californica SIZE: TO 6 FT. WIDE (1.8 M)
Bat rays prey on clams, shrimp, worms and other invertebrates that live in the mud. Flapping their wings to clear away mud, rays suck up their prey, crushing the shells with their strong jaws and hard, flat teeth. In summer, bat rays enter sloughs and bays where they give birth to live young. It's a trait they share with several other members of the shark family.

Pipefish with eelgrass

Syngnathus leptorhynchus with *Zostera marina*
SIZE: PIPEFISH TO 13 IN. (33 CM)
EELGRASS TO 3 FT. (91 CM)
With its long and thin, green body, a pipefish blends in well with the eelgrass blades it lives in. It even sways back and forth with the currents like eelgrass does. Eelgrass, unlike most flowering plants, lives with its roots in mud under the water. Its matted roots trap sediments, helping to keep the mud in place and providing a stable home for many animals.

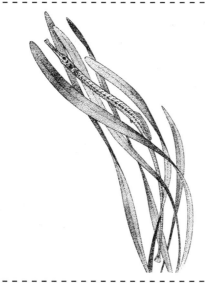

Brown pelican

Pelecanus occidentalis SIZE: TO 7 FT. WINGSPAN (2 M)
Thousands of pelicans visit Elkhorn Slough in summer and fall. In late fall, they migrate south to Mexico and South America where they build saucer-shaped nests on the ground or in trees and raise two to three young. In the 1960s, heavy use of the pesticide DDT nearly killed all the brown pelicans. Today, DDT is banned in the United States. But its use in Mexico and other countries along with habitat loss within the pelican's range are still threats.

Red fox

Vulpes fulva SIZE: TO 3.5 FT. (106 CM)

A red fox stalks its prey at night, feeding on ground-nesting birds, their eggs and small animals. During the day it returns to its home in the uplands, a den dug down in the ground. Many people are concerned about red foxes at Elkhorn Slough. Unlike native gray foxes, red foxes were brought to the slough by people. Without natural predators, the red fox's population grows unchecked. And as red fox numbers grow, populations of its prey decline.

Great blue heron

Ardea herodias SIZE: TO 6 FT. WINGSPAN (1.8 M)

Great blue herons live year-round at Elkhorn Slough. They depend on Elkhorn Slough to eat, rest and raise their young. Look for them standing still in shallow water, quietly waiting to snatch and eat small fishes that swim by. In early spring, great blue herons build nests in the tops of trees. Made of twigs and leaves, each nest shelters three to five bluish-green eggs. Both the male and female incubate the eggs which take about two months to hatch.

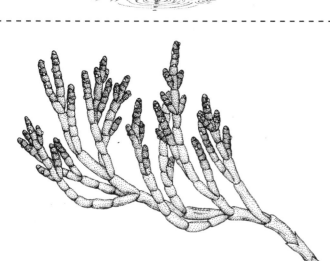

Pickleweed

Salicornia virginica SIZE: TO 25 IN. (63 CM)

This plant can withstand salty conditions that would cause other plants to wither and die. Pickleweed draws the slough's saltwater into its stems and stores the extra salt in the tips of the stems. In fall, the stems turn color, becoming orange or rosy red. Then they wither and drop off, taking the stored salt with them.

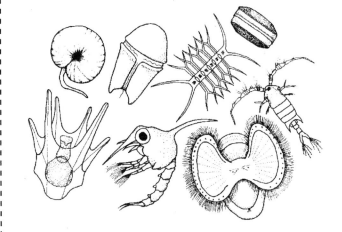

Plankton

(Plant plankton, top row from left: two dinoflagellates, chain diatom, diatom. Animal plankton, bottom row: sea urchin larva, crab larva, snail larva, copepod.) Plankton are plants and animals, mostly tiny, that drift on ocean currents instead of swimming. Plant plankton form the first link in many of the ocean's food chains. Animal plankton eat these tiny plants. Filter-feeders like clams and sand crabs eat both kinds of plankton.

Skeleton shrimp

Caprella californica SIZE: TO 1.5 IN. (4 CM)
You have to look closely to find skeleton shrimp. Their small, clear, sticklike bodies blend in well with the eelgrass where they live. They cling to the plants with three pairs of legs, and use their clawlike "arms" for grabbing food, fending off predators and cleaning themselves. A skeleton shrimp eats whatever it can. It feeds on smaller plants and animals and scavenges for other bits of food.

Fat innkeeper worm

Urechis caupo SIZE: TO 20 IN. (51 CM)
An innkeeper worm digs a U-shaped tunnel in the mud. At one end, it attaches a mucous net that it secretes from special glands. Slowly pulsing its body, the innkeeper pumps water through its tunnel. As water flows through, the net traps tiny plankton floating in the water. When the net is full, the innkeeper eats both it and the trapped food. Worms, crabs and even a certain fish share the tunnel, eating anything the innkeeper misses.

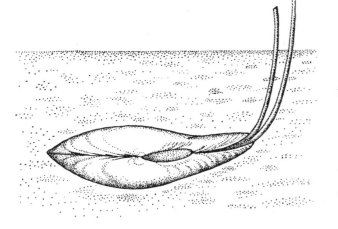

Bent-nosed clam

Macoma nasuta SIZE: TO 2.5 IN. (6 CM)

Using its muscular foot, this clam digs about six inches down into the mud. It rocks back and forth as it digs, like a coin sinking in water. When it finally settles, it lies horizontally, not vertically, like most clams. To eat and breathe, it sticks a tube up to the mud's surface. Like a vacuum cleaner, the clam sucks down tiny particles, mostly the remains of plants and animals, along with sand and grit. Then it sorts the food from the muck.

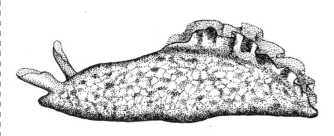

Sea hare

Aplysia californica SIZE: TO 16 IN. (41 CM)

A sea hare glides along the muddy bottom, searching for algae to eat. With its filelike tongue, called a radula, it scrapes up its food, eating nearly 10 percent of its body weight a day. An adult sea hare is both a male and a female, but it must mate with another sea hare. After mating, it lays strings of greenish eggs that look like spaghetti. Each string contains up to a million eggs.

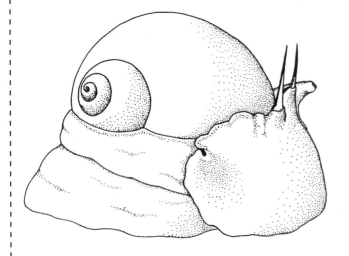

Moon snail

Polinices lewisii SIZE: TO 5 IN. (13 CM)

A moon snail plows slowly through the sand, hunting for clams. When it finds one, the snail wraps its huge foot around the clam's shell. It rasps a hole in the shell with its filelike tongue, called a radula, and softens the shell with a special liquid. When the hole is big enough, the snail slurps up the clam's soft insides.

The Kelp Forest

What Is a Kelp Forest?

Giant kelp plants form submarine forests in the cool waters of many of the world's oceans. Extensive forests grow along the Pacific coast of North America. Beautiful, biologically complex communities, they provide food and shelter for a rich array of plants and animals. They're also a very important economic and recreational resource for fishermen and divers in places like Monterey Bay, California.

During World War I, California kelp forests were harvested as a source of potash for gunpowder. Today, giant kelp is harvested for a gel called algin. Algin is used in many products including foods like ice cream, pharmaceuticals such as tablets (to help them dissolve) and cosmetics and clothing (to keep the color dyes from bleeding). Between 100,000 and 170,000 tons of giant kelp are harvested annually in California.

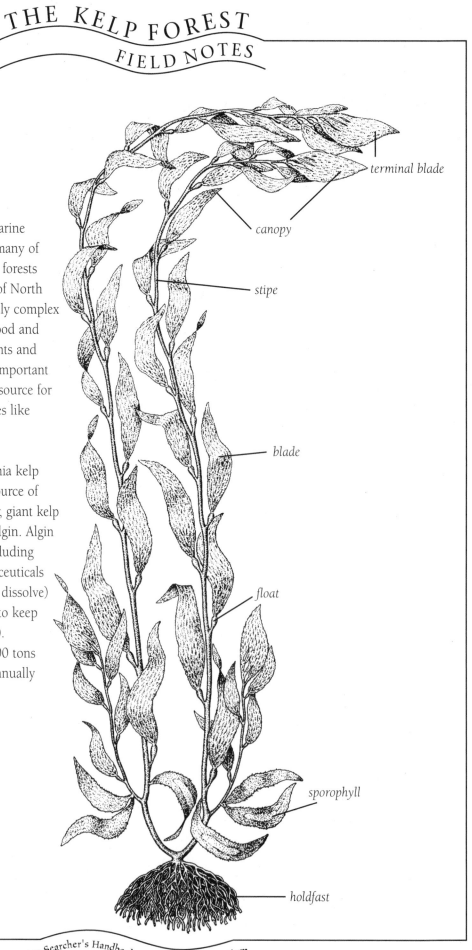

terminal blade

canopy

stipe

blade

float

sporophyll

holdfast

The giant kelp plant

Kelp refers to large brown algae in the division Phaeophyta. Like other algae, giant kelp has no true roots, stems, leaves or flowers. A single frond can live for more than six months.

The huge plants you see in the bay are only half of the kelp's life cycle. These large plants, called sporophytes, release spores that swim to the bottom and grow into tiny male and female plants (gametophytes) which carry out the other half of the cycle. The tiny male plants release sperm that fertilize the females' eggs. The resulting embryos grow into huge giant kelp plants (sporophytes) and the cycle begins again. It takes about a year for the kelp to complete the reproductive cycle.

Giant kelp grows best in areas with rocky bottoms, plenty of light and enough water motion to keep nutrients circulating around the plant. Interactions with other organisms also affect where kelp grows. First, kelp must compete with plants and animals for space to settle and grow. Then, as it grows toward the surface, kelp competes with nearby plants for light. At all stages of its life, kelp must survive being grazed by sea urchins, abalones, other invertebrates and some fishes.

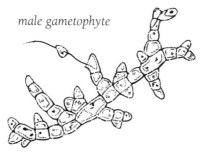

male gametophyte

A male gametophyte releases sperm that fertilize egg cells on the female gametophyte. Once fertilized, the egg cell grows into a young sporophyte, and a new generation begins.

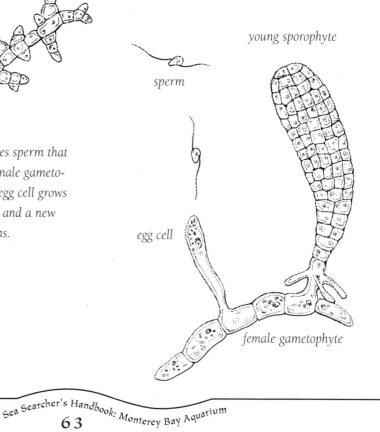

young sporophyte

sperm

egg cell

female gametophyte

The kelp forest community

A kelp forest has a greater variety and higher density of plants and animals than almost any other ocean community. This is largely because its complex physical structure offers more kinds of homes than homogeneous areas like beaches. Like trees, kelp plants provide a variety of living spaces. Some organisms swim in the canopy, and others live on the fronds, between the stipes or in the holdfast.

Another reason this community is rich and diverse is that kelp is an abundant, continuous source of food. Some animals, like turban snails, graze directly on the growing plant, but many animals (like abalones, sea urchins and bat stars) feed on detached fronds that have drifted to the bottom. Drift kelp that isn't eaten is decomposed by bacteria into small particles called detritus. The detritus is filtered from the water by filter-feeders, like sponges, or ingested from the sediment by deposit-feeders, like some sea cucumbers. In turn, many of these animals are eaten by predators including crabs, rockfishes and sea stars.

About 90 percent of the kelp produced in the forest each year ends up on the beach or in deep water. Only about 10 percent gets eaten within the kelp forest itself.

Sea cucumber

Adaptations for kelp forest life

All kelp forest plants and animals have similar basic needs: they must find food, reproduce, avoid being eaten and adjust to the physical environment. We study characteristics like mouthparts, shape and locomotion to tell what such adaptations are for and what role (producer, predator, herbivore or planktivore) the plant or animal plays in the community.

Look at the illustrations of animals in the Kelp Forest Field Guide. A sea otter's sleek body is adapted to move through the water. What about the orange sea cucumber? A planktivore, its finely divided tentacles are adapted to filter plankton and detritus from the water; the soft body is adapted to fit into rocky cracks and crevices.

Making similar studies of other kelp forest plants and animals will help you understand the roles and relationships of organisms in the kelp forest community.

Growing Tall

MATERIALS
- Six containers or cups (the bottoms of milk cartons work great)
- Potting soil
- Bean seeds
- Graph paper
- Measuring cup
- Pencil

Grow bean seeds under different conditions to see when plants grow best. Take a guess before you start your experiment: do you think seeds grow best with lots of sunlight or little sunlight? How much water helps plants grow tallest? Now experiment to find out!

With the help of an adult, use a pencil to poke a hole in the bottom of each container. Fill the containers with equal amounts of soil, then plant the bean seeds according to the directions on the package. Plant each seed at the same depth and in the same position. Give them each a measured amount of water . . . enough so that a few drops of water drain out the hole.

Put two of your bean plants in a dark room and two in a sunlit room. Give these four plants the measured amount of water during their growth. Put the remaining two plants in the sun, but only water them half as much as the other plants. Measure your plants and record their heights on a graph. Which plants grow faster? Why? What other experiments could you try? (Remember to guess what will happen first, then try the experiment to prove or disprove your guess.) What do your bean plants need to survive? (They need sunlight, water, nutrients, protection from bad weather.) What do you think an ocean plant like giant kelp needs to survive? What parts of the plant fulfill these needs?

How is a kelp forest similar to a forest on land? How is it different? How are trees important to the inhabitants of a forest? How is kelp important to the inhabitants of a kelp forest?

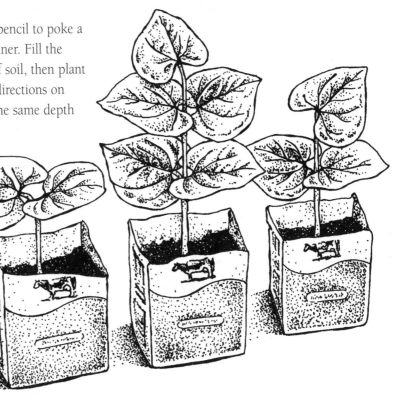

Producers on Land and in the Sea

MATERIALS
- Two sheets of paper
- Pencil

Take a walk in your backyard, school yard or through a park. Draw a map of the area, then draw a producer (plant), herbivore (plant-eater), carnivore (meat-eater), scavenger and decomposer that live there. On another sheet of paper, draw a picture of a kelp forest with a producer (kelp), herbivore (sea urchin), carnivore (sea otter), scavenger (crab) and decomposer (bacteria). Compare your two food chains. What happens to an ecosystem when its food chain is disrupted? What kinds of things disrupt food chains and webs? What can you do to help prevent these disruptions from taking place?

Take a Dive

MATERIALS
- Favorite drawing materials
- Paper

Pretend you're scuba diving in a kelp forest. Write and illustrate a log of what you see and do during your dive.

Sun

Kelp

Abalone

Sea otter

Sea urchin

Do You Eat Kelp?

Did you know that you probably eat kelp and other seaweeds? On your next visit to the market, look for products with ingredients like algin, alginic acid, carageenan and nori. If you need help getting started, look at the ingredients in toothpaste, ice cream and puddings. What are other ways people use kelp? (People use kelp for commercial products, sport fishing in kelp forests, diving, harvesting and industrial products.)

What's the difference between a renewable resource and a non-renewable resource? Are kelp forests renewable or non-renewable? (Kelp grows very quickly and is a renewable resource.) Since kelp is renewable, does that mean we can harvest as much as we want? What are some non-renewable resources? (Oil is a non-renewable resource.) Do you think people should rely on non-renewable resources? What are the alternatives?

Leaf Rubbing Note Cards

MATERIALS
- A variety of leaves, grasses and fern fronds
- Paper, folded in half or cut in half and folded in quarters to make note cards
- Crayons with the paper peeled off
- Newspaper

Collect a variety of leaves. Look for large ones and small ones, wide ones and skinny ones, pointed ones and round ones. Layer the newspapers on your work area; the more you have, the better your rubbings will look. Place the leaves on the newspaper and lay your note card paper on top. Using the side of a crayon (instead of the pointed ends), rub over the leaf. Create designs by using different leaves and by rubbing hard in some places and gently in others. When you're done, return the leaves to your yard. Compare your leaves to the illustration of the giant kelp plant on page 62. How are the plants the same? How are they different?

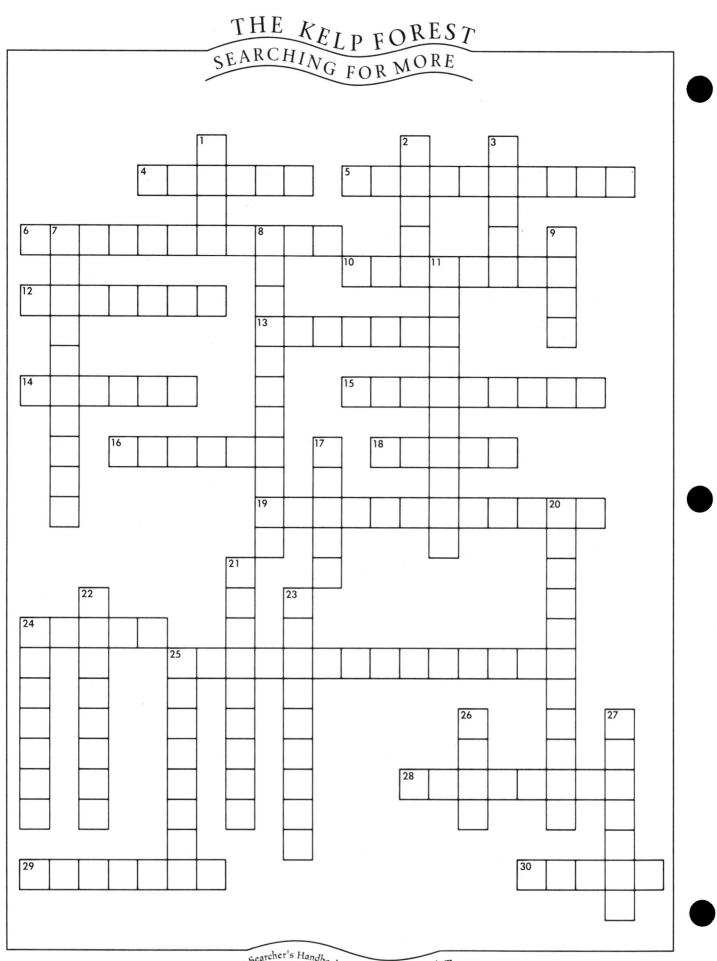

Kelp Forest Crossword Puzzle

ACROSS

4. of the sea
5. how barnacles eat
6. scientific name of giant kelp
10. an animal that kills and eats animals
12. where a plant or animal lives
13. decorator crabs are bottom-dwelling, or

_____

14. the top layer of the kelp forest
15. all of the plants and animals living in a specific area
16. a spiny sea _____ lives at the bottom of the kelp forest
18. a kelp stipe and the attached blades
19. an animal without a backbone
24. abbreviation for self-contained underwater breathing apparatus
25. how green plants use sunlight to produce food
28. the part of the seaweed that attaches it to the seafloor
29. a large flat snail that eats kelp and is a preferred prey of sea otters
30. the name of simple non-seed-bearing plants

DOWN

1. an animal that is killed and eaten by a predator
2. the leaflike part of a seaweed
3. _____ seaweed: a piece of seaweed that has broken its attachment and floats freely with the ocean currents
7. a characteristic (body part, behavior or other) that helps a plant or animal survive
8. many hermit crabs live in empty _____
_____ shells

9. a predatory crustacean
11. organism that causes the decay of dead plant and animal matter
17. SCUBA _____: a person adapted to spend time under water
20. of the land
21. marine mammals found in the kelp forests off the coast of Monterey
22. the minerals giant kelp needs for growth (singular)
23. life forms that produce their own food through photosynthesis
24. common name for large ocean plants
25. tiny plants and animals that swim weakly or drift with ocean currents
26. any of the large brown seaweeds, like _Macrocystis_
27. common sea star found in kelp forests

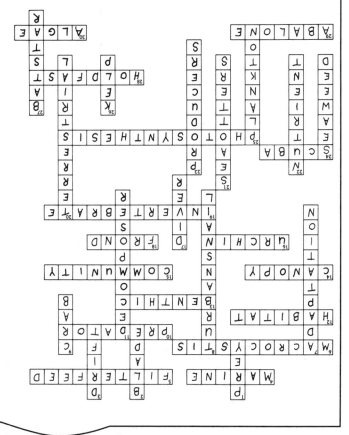

Sea otter

Enhydra lutris SIZE: TO 4.9 FT. (1.5 M)

Sea otters live in kelp forests, often wrapping themselves in the fronds before they sleep. They are equipped for life at sea with webbed hind feet and a thick, insulating fur coat. Otters eat abalones, crabs, urchins, sea stars, snails and other shellfish. To break the hard shells, otters pound them with rocks.

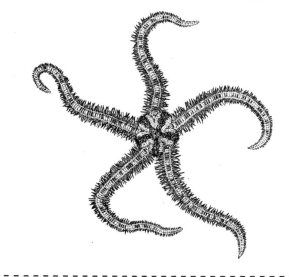

Brittle star

Ophiothrix spiculata

SIZE: TO 5.7 IN. (14.4 CM)

Brittle stars hide among rocks and in the rootlike kelp holdfasts, anchored into cracks by their long spines. Their delicate arms break easily, but also grow back quickly. Brittle stars catch suspended food particles by waving their arms through the water. Small tube feet on each arm transfer the food to the mouth.

Red abalone

Haliotis rufescens SIZE: TO 11.8 IN. (30 CM)

Red abalone live in crevices, rarely moving far from a chosen spot on the rock. The holes in the shell are outlets for water circulation. These abalone catch passing seaweed for food. When the tentacles sense a large piece of drifting kelp, the abalone rears toward it, then grabs the seaweed with its big foot.

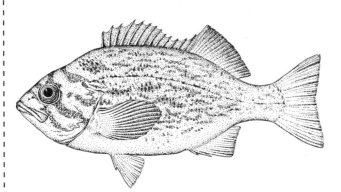

Blue rockfish

Sebastes mystinus SIZE: TO 21 IN. (53 CM)

Schools of blue rockfish swim among the kelp plants. Sport fishermen often catch these fish, but they must be careful when they do: rockfishes have poisonous spines on some of their fins. Blue rockfish eat small floating animals like shrimps and jellies.

Decorator crab

Loxorhynchus crispatus SIZE: TO 3.5 IN. (8.8 CM)

A decorator crab camouflages its shell with algae, sponges and other things that grow on local rocks. When the crab sheds the shell for a new one, it has to redecorate. Often, the crab will transfer material from the old shell to the new. Decorator crabs eat algae, sea urchins, small crustaceans and sponges.

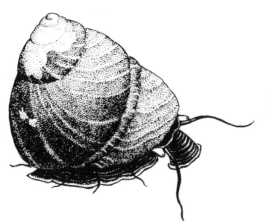

Brown turban snail

Tegula brunnea SIZE: TO 1 IN. (2.5 CM)

Brown turban snails live on kelp plants, most often on the upper blades. Predators like the sea star live on the seafloor below, so the turban snail is safer up high in the canopy. Kelp provides lunch as well as a living-place for the turban snail. The snails rasp away the algae with their filelike tongues.

Sheephead

Semicossyphus pulcher SIZE: TO 3 FT. (91 CM)
Sheephead swim above rocky areas. These fish are all born female, but turn into males when they grow to about 12 inches. They also turn color, from red to red-and-black with white chins. Sheephead eat snails, crabs, urchins and other shellfish. They're good to eat, so divers often catch them.

Cabezon

Scorpaenichthys marmoratus
SIZE: TO 3.25 FT. (99 CM)
Like their relatives, the small tidepool sculpins, cabezons live on the bottom in rocky areas. When they sit still, their waving fins and mottled color blend in with the surrounding seaweed. Cabezons eat invertebrates like crabs and snails, and some fishes. They swallow abalones whole, then spit out the shells.

Gumboot chiton

Cryptochiton stelleri SIZE: TO 12 IN. (30 CM)
The gumboot chiton is the largest chiton in the world. It lives on the kelp forest floor, clinging to rocks with its single large foot. It looks like half a football, but is related to snails and clams. Its eight shells are inside, like a skeleton. A gumboot chiton eats mostly red seaweeds, rasping with a filelike tongue.

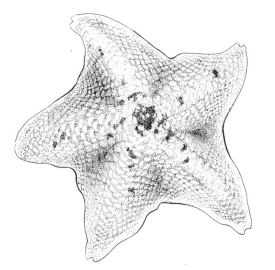

Bat star
Patiria miniata SIZE: TO 8 IN. (20 CM)
Bat stars live on the kelp forest floor. They eat seaweeds and small animals, and scavenge dead animals on the bottom. A bat star's stomach comes out of its mouth and covers its food to eat. The stomach can feel around on the seafloor for bits of food.

Sea cucumber
Parastichopus californicus SIZE: TO 16 IN. (40 CM)
Sea cucumbers creep slowly across the kelp forest floor. Relatives of the sea stars, they use hundreds of tiny suction-cup feet called "tube feet" to move. The tentacles around a sea cucumber's mouth are also a type of tube foot. The sea cucumber brushes the tentacles across the seafloor as it moves, collecting organic particles and stuffing them into its mouth.

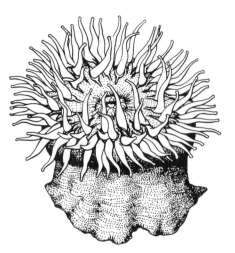

Fish-eating anemone
Tealia piscivora SIZE: TO 8 IN. (20 CM)
This anemone snares shrimps and small fishes. Its stinging tentacles shoot thousands of tiny harpoons into the prey to hold it. A poison from the harpoons stuns the prey. After making a catch, the anemone stuffs the meal into its mouth, then closes up to digest it.

SEARCHING SEA HABITATS

The Open Sea

What Is the Open Sea?

Moving away from the shallow waters along the coast and into the deeper water of the ocean, one travels through the open sea— a vast world with no walls. In this habitat, changes in the physical and chemical characteristics of the water create boundaries. These boundaries, seemingly invisible, divide the open sea into different water masses, each with its own characteristic plants and animals. The residents here sense differences in temperature, salinity, available sunlight and dissolved chemicals or nutrients. As the seasons change and their water mass moves, these organisms travel with the water mass that suits them best.

Life in the open sea is divided into two groups: drifters (plankton) and swimmers (nekton). Plankton are weak swimmers, carried mainly by currents. A diverse group, they range from microscopic plants and animals to large jellies. Nekton include fishes, whales, sea turtles and squid. They travel great distances to find food. With very different lifestyles, both groups are well-adapted for life in the open sea.

Leatherback sea turtle

Plankton

A different world

Plants and animals in this habitat live in a world of water. They don't have to contend with hard surfaces, gravity or the threat of drying out. But life here presents different problems.

Because sunlight and their richest food supplies are in the surface waters, plants and plankton eaters must stay near the surface to survive. To accomplish this, microscopic plants and animals develop elaborate structures to slow their rates of sinking, while many fishes have air-filled swimbladders which support them in the water. Whales rely on blubber or fat for the same purpose. Without places to hide, animals of the open sea must also avoid predators. Many species of zooplankton come to the surface waters at night to feed on small, single-celled plants. During the day, they sink to deeper waters to avoid being seen by predatory fishes or birds. Many fishes school for protection. Their safety comes from the larger and more threatening appearance presented by many fishes rather than by just one. Schooling also causes greater confusion for a predator that's trying to find, follow and catch a single animal in a large group.

Some animals, like jellies, have virtually invisible gelatinous bodies. Others, like tuna, rely on countershading coloration (light on the bottom, dark on top) to be less visible. Viewed from above, their bodies blend in with the ocean depths; while from below their light undersides blend with bright surface waters.

Floating pastures

Large "slicks" of microscopic plants (called phytoplankton) are found in patches near the ocean's surface. Tiny, but present in unimaginable numbers, phytoplankton support virtually all life in the oceans.

These plants need sun to grow and photosynthesize so it's vital that they remain in the upper waters where sunlight can penetrate. A small body size, irregular body shape and long fibers help slow their sinking. Worldwide, their photosynthesizing produces most of the oxygen in the ocean. Since all animals—including ourselves—need oxygen to survive, healthy phytoplankton and a clean ocean are important to us. Polluting the ocean harms them,

and without them, we'd be short of a gas essential to our survival.

Like all plants, phytoplankton also need nutrients to survive. Phytoplankton absorb nitrates, phosphates and other nutrients directly from their surroundings. When the nutrients are used up, the plankton must swim, sink or float to a new patch of nutrient-rich water. Sometimes nutrients are replaced through the remixing of water due to waves, currents and upwelling. Eventually the plankton die and sink to the bottom where they become a valuable food source for deep sea creatures.

Animal drifters

Nearly every group of animals has representatives who spend at least part of their lives adrift in the ocean. Animal drifters (called zooplankton) vary from microscopic organisms to large jellies. Some are herbivores, grazing on the phytoplankton, while others are voracious predators of planktonic larvae. Still others, like jellies, are passive predators waiting for a fish or shrimp to become tangled in their tentacles.

Purple-striped jelly

Yellowfin tuna

Drifting provides a means to disperse young. Many, like crabs, barnacles and some fishes, produce planktonic larvae. Their young develop adrift at sea. Mortality is high among planktonic larvae—many are eaten by larger predators, others are swept far out to sea. But eggs and sperm are small and require little energy to produce. The parents would invest far more energy if they cared for the larvae until they were fully developed.

The swimmers

Nekton, the open sea's powerful swimmers, face the same buoyancy and predation challenges that plankton do, but they meet these challenges in different ways.

Nekton are built to chase down prey and avoid predators. Tuna have muscular, torpedo-shaped bodies and crescent-shaped tails. Streamlined and powerful, they can travel at speeds of up to 40 miles per hour! When tuna swim fast, their fins lie flat against their body, reducing both drag and turbulence. Even their eyes fit smoothly into the outline of their bodies.

Swimming takes energy—which these active swimmers get by eating large amounts of food. Adults seek areas of the ocean where food is abundant and migrate seasonally to seek out and stay with these water masses. Since conditions in these water masses usually aren't suitable for larvae or young, adults migrate to other areas at certain times of the year to spawn or give birth. Gray whales migrate up and down the California coast every year, traveling between their Alaskan feeding grounds in summer and their winter nursery lagoons off Baja California.

Responsible for the open sea

With a growing human population, an increase in consumption by some people and advancing technology, people are having a greater impact on the ocean's inhabitants and water quality. In the Monterey Bay area of California, sardines, anchovies, tuna, gray whales and sea otters have all been overfished or overhunted. The habitat is also being harmed by the accumulation of chemicals and trash. Chemicals, oils, herbicides and pesticides from our homes, yards, streets, factories and farms enter the ocean through sewage treatment plants and run-off from storms, rivers or melting snow. Scientists are still learning what effects these chemicals have on the open sea habitat. They may threaten the plankton that support complex food webs with oxygen and food. Trash has more obvious effects. Plastic bags kill sea turtles who swallow them, believing they're jellies. And sea birds and mammals have been found starved to death, entangled by plastic soda can rings or fishing lines . . . or drowned, entangled in fishing nets.

Laws regulate how many fishes can be collected and which type of substances may be released into the sea. We can help keep the sea healthy by learning more about it as well as coastal habitats and by following current events in the news, supporting effective environmental legislation, respecting and obeying fishing regulations, keeping trash off of our beaches and safely disposing of toxic chemicals.

Pacific white-sided dolphins

Design a Drifter

M A T E R I A L S
• Variety of materials including corks, toothpicks, clay, pipe
cleaners, paper clips, twist-ties, rubber bands,
coffee stirrers, biodegradable packaging
pellets and metal washers

Use a variety of materials to create a
drifter that lives at sea.
Remember, your drifter
must be submerged.
It can't float at the
surface because it'll
get sunburned or
be eaten by predators;
and your drifter can't sink
because it needs sunlight to grow,
or perhaps it feeds on plants that live
at the surface.

What Does a Jelly Feel Like?

M A T E R I A L S
• 1 envelope of
unflavored gelatin
• 1 1/2 cups cold
water
• Bowl
• Plastic baggie
(sandwich size)

A bag full of jello feels a
lot like a jelly that lives
in the sea. Make a
batch of jello and chill
it in a bag to make your
own jelly at home.

Dissolve gelatin in $^1/_4$
cup cold water, let
stand for two minutes.
Put the gelatin mixture
in microwave on high
for 30 seconds, stir the
mixture thoroughly,
then let it stand again for two minutes.
Add 1$^1/_4$ cups cold water and mix
thoroughly. Pour mixture into a plastic
baggie and chill.

*Make a bag full of jello and see what a
jelly feels like to the touch.*

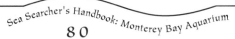

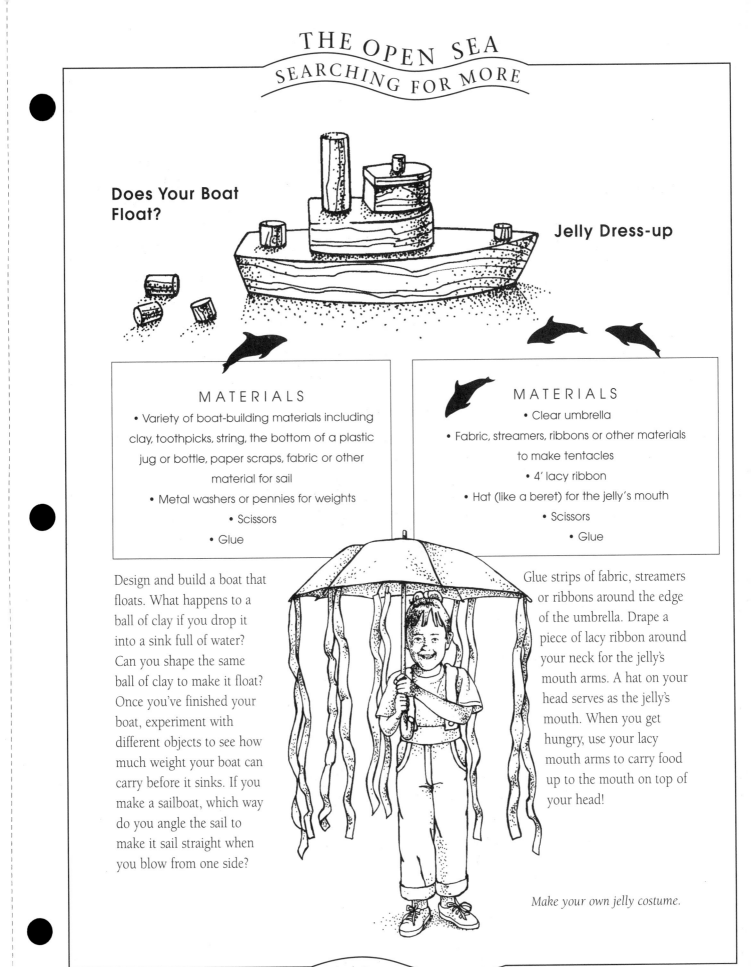

Does Your Boat Float?

Jelly Dress-up

MATERIALS

- Variety of boat-building materials including clay, toothpicks, string, the bottom of a plastic jug or bottle, paper scraps, fabric or other material for sail
- Metal washers or pennies for weights
- Scissors
- Glue

MATERIALS

- Clear umbrella
- Fabric, streamers, ribbons or other materials to make tentacles
- 4' lacy ribbon
- Hat (like a beret) for the jelly's mouth
- Scissors
- Glue

Design and build a boat that floats. What happens to a ball of clay if you drop it into a sink full of water? Can you shape the same ball of clay to make it float? Once you've finished your boat, experiment with different objects to see how much weight your boat can carry before it sinks. If you make a sailboat, which way do you angle the sail to make it sail straight when you blow from one side?

Glue strips of fabric, streamers or ribbons around the edge of the umbrella. Drape a piece of lacy ribbon around your neck for the jelly's mouth arms. A hat on your head serves as the jelly's mouth. When you get hungry, use your lacy mouth arms to carry food up to the mouth on top of your head!

Make your own jelly costume.

Jelly Windsock

MATERIALS
- Two coat hangers
- Wire cutters
- Piece of fabric (size depends on how big you'd like to make your windsock)
- Measuring tape
- Strips of fabric, ribbons or streamers
- Scissors
- Glue
- String

How is your jelly windsock similar to and different from a real jelly in the ocean? Do jellies move the same in the wind as they do in the water? Why or why not?

Cut the two coat hangers and reshape them to make two circles of equal size. Measure the circumference of the circles, then cut a piece of fabric one inch wider than the circumference. The length of your windsock depends on how long you'd like your windsock to be. Remember to add one inch to the top and one inch to the bottom to fold over the wire hanger. Wrap the top end of your fabric around one of the wire circles, fold over about an inch of fabric and glue the fabric together, enclosing the wire hanger. Do the same at the bottom of your fabric with the other wire circle to create a cylinder. Glue strips of fabric, streamers or ribbons along the bottom edge of the cylinder to make tentacles. Fasten the string to the top wire hanger and hang your jelly!

Purple-striped jellies

Snazzy Squid Costume

MATERIALS

- Foam (check the Yellow Pages for local foam or mattress stores): 54" x 76" sheet (double bed size) of 1"-thick foam for a child's costume
- 12' of 36"-wide butcher paper
- 2' of 3/4" Velcro
- 2/3 yard (2'x 4' square) of black chiffon fabric
- Clear quart-size plastic bag
- 2' of string
- Spray or craft paint - 1 can each of black and silver
- Contact cement or spray adhesive
- Highlighter pen
- Scissors
- Rubber gloves
- Balloon

To make your Snazzy Squid suit

It'll help if you read all the directions and study the illustrations before constructing your squid suit. Find a comfortable, well-ventilated place to work and have clean-up materials handy. Read and follow the health warnings on the glue and paint containers. Plan on spending about three hours making this costume.

1. On the butcher paper or newsprint, draw a grid with six-inch squares (an enlarged version of the grid on page 85). Enlarge the pattern pieces onto your grid, drawing one square at a time. Cut out the pieces, lay them on the foam and outline them with the highlighter pen. Cut out the foam body parts.

2. Mantle: glue the scratchy side of three 4-inch pieces of Velcro along one side of the mantle at point A. Glue the three matching fuzzy pieces along the mantle's other side. Glue the scratchy side of a 4-inch piece of Velcro to the inside of the mantle at the neck at point B. Cut out the arm holes.

3. Siphon: glue the sides of the siphon (D) together to form a tube. (You can use rubber bands to hold the tube closed while it dries.) Glue the fuzzy side of the 4-inch piece of Velcro to the outside of the siphon at point E.

4. Headband-of-arms: glue the narrow ends of the feeding tentacles (G) to the inside center of the headband-of-arms at point G. (The round ends should point upward in the same direction as the pointed ends of the arms.) Glue a 4-inch piece of Velcro to each end of the headband at point H.

5. Paint a black line to separate the mantle from the lateral fins. Decorate the mantle and lateral fins with 2-inch diameter silver and black circles. Paint the arms and the round ends of the feeding tentacles with 2-inch diameter black circles to represent suction cups.

6. Ink sac: stuff the piece of black chiffon into the quart-size plastic bag. Tie the opening closed with the string.

Squid notes

A squid swims through the ocean, sometimes darting with quick bursts of speed, other times slowly cruising along. It hunts for small fishes and shrimp, which it suddenly snatches with its longest tentacles. When danger threatens, it can release a squirt of ink, stored in a sac inside its body, to cloud a predator's view. Or it can jet away with a quick burst of speed by contracting its muscular mantle to force water out through its narrow siphon.

(To show how a squid jets away, help your child blow up a balloon. Then let the balloon go without tying a knot. Air forced through the balloon's narrow opening is similar to water forced through the squid's siphon. A squid can control its direction by pointing its siphon forward to go backward and vice versa.)

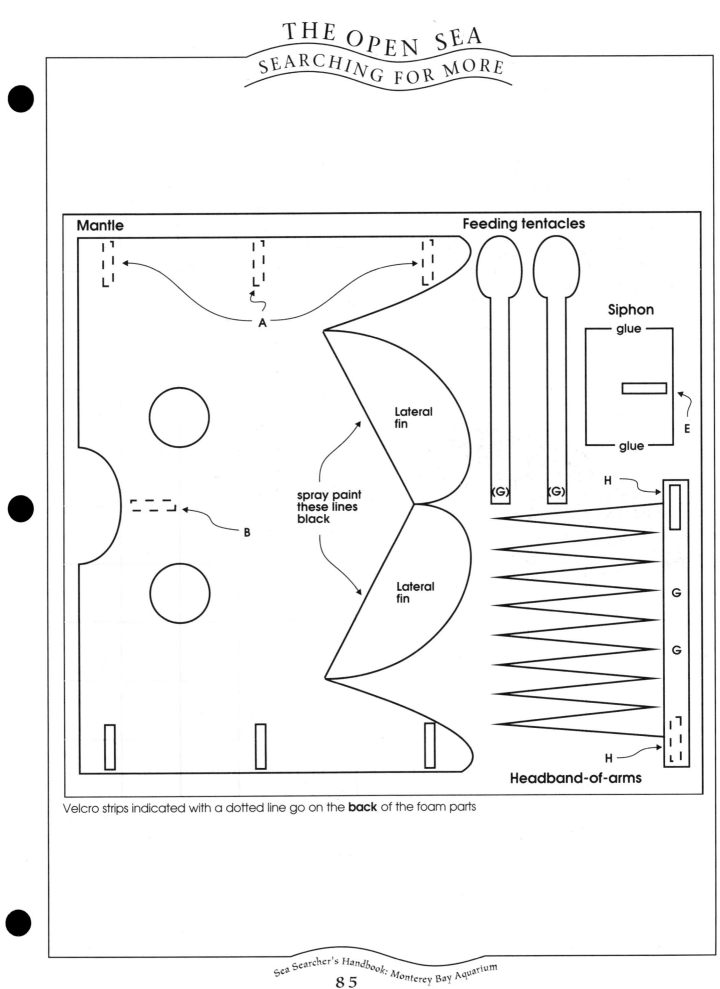

Mantle

Feeding tentacles

A

Siphon

glue

glue

E

B

Lateral fin

spray paint these lines black

Lateral fin

(G)   (G)

H

G

G

H

Headband-of-arms

Velcro strips indicated with a dotted line go on the **back** of the foam parts

Plankton

(Plant plankton, top row from left: two dinoflagellates, chain diatom, diatom. Animal plankton, bottom row: sea urchin larva, crab larva, snail larva, copepod.) Plankton are plants and animals, mostly tiny, that drift on ocean currents instead of swimming. Plant plankton form the first link in many of the ocean's food chains. Animal plankton eat these tiny plants. Filter-feeders like clams and sand crabs eat both kinds of plankton.

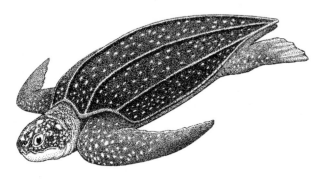

Leatherback sea turtle
Dermochelys coriacea coriacea
SIZE: TO 6 FT. (1.8 M)

Sea turtles eat jellies. When plastic bags and balloons get in the ocean, they look like jellies. Sometimes turtles eat the plastic by mistake, then they choke and starve.

Purple-striped jelly
Pelagia colorata
SIZE: TO 2.5 FT. DIAMETER OF BELL (80 CM)

In certain seasons, when the currents run just right, purple-striped jellies mysteriously appear near the shores of Monterey Bay, California. When the jellies arrive, it's wise to keep your distance (their sting isn't fatal, but it can be painful). Since divers have seen ocean sunfish eating these jellies, we know some fishes must be immune to the sting.

Pacific white-sided dolphin

Lagenorhynchus obliquidens

SIZE: TO 6.5 FT (2M)

Bounding through the open waters of the northern Pacific Ocean, white-sided dolphins travel in groups that can number in the hundreds. They swim with other dolphins and sea lions, sometimes leaping from the water in spirited somersaults. Dolphins need to keep in touch with each other, and each dolphin makes its own sounds. High-pitched squeaks, clicks and whistles help a dolphin call to its family pod.

Yellowfin tuna

Thunnus albacares SIZE: TO 6.5 FT (2M)

Sleek, streamlined and fast, yellowfin tuna travel the Indian, Pacific and Atlantic oceans. Local laws can't protect these international travelers from overfishing. This makes the problem of tuna conservation a global one—which means we need to find global solutions.

Blue shark

Prionace glauca SIZE: TO 12.5 FT (3.8M)

Blue sharks are generally found near the surface of the water. Despite their large size, these sharks feed mostly on fishes, squid and tiny shrimplike krill, but they may eat practically anything that comes their way.

SEARCHING SEA HABITATS

The Deep Sea Canyon

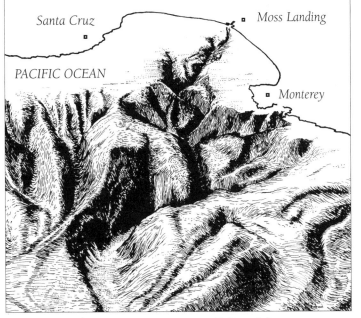

Monterey Bay submarine canyon off the California coast

What Is the Deep Sea?

Cold and dark, the deep sea is the largest, but least known, region on earth. The deep-seafloor extends under water from the edge of the continental shelf, across broad plains and down into trenches seven miles deep. The deep sea covers about 60 percent of the earth's surface, but we know more about the moon than we know about the ocean depths.

Why do we know so little? It's difficult and expensive to sample miles below the surface. Oceanographers go to sea aboard huge research vessels equipped with echo-sounders, expensive deep-water dredges, traps and submersible vehicles.

Some scientists study the midwater fishes and invertebrates thatswim or hover in the water; others focus on thebenthic animals living on the ocean bottom. Midwater or bottom, only small areas of the ocean can be sampled at a time. Sampling lets us know about where different animals live and how they have adapted to the low temperatures, high pressure and darkness of the deep sea.

Monterey Canyon

Just offshore in Monterey Bay lies a canyon that's twice as deep and one-third the length of the Grand Canyon. The huge chasm cuts the bay nearly in half, sloping down from a depth of about 60 feet (18 meters) at Moss Landing to nearly 12,000 feet (3,656 meters) at its end 60 miles (97 kilometers) out to sea. Because of the Monterey Canyon, we have deep sea habitats close to shore.

Temperature

Try a quick dip in Monterey Bay on a sunny day. The water temperatures here range from 50° to 60° F (10° to 15° C), shocking to the hardiest of swimmers. Even on the warmest day, the bay can absorb a lot of radiant energy and heat from the sun without much change in temperature.

Monterey Bay is so cold at the surface that it's hard to imagine the deep layers as colder yet. But 300 feet (91 meters) down, the ocean has cooled down another 10 degrees.

Deep sea shrimp

Below 3,000 feet (914 meters), the water cools gradually to just above freezing and remains bitterly cold throughout the year without any seasonal change.

Pressure

Scientists who use submersible vehicles sometimes attach Styrofoam cups to the vehicle's exterior to demonstrate how pressure increases with depth in the ocean. On the surface, at an atmospheric pressure of 14.7 pounds per square inch, a Styrofoam cup stands about four inches tall. As the submersible sinks down into the ocean depths, the scientist can watch the coffee cup gradually shrink as the pressure permanently compresses the Styrofoam. Below 3,000 feet (914 meters), under pressure 100 times greater than that at the surface, the Styrofoam cup has shriveled to about one half of its original size. In the deepest ocean trenches, pressure is a crushing 1,000 times surface atmospheric pressure.

Pressure probably limits where many ocean animals can survive. Fishes with slow adjusting gas bladders would explode if they migrated upward into reduced pressure. Changes in pressure may also affect deep sea animals by speeding up or slowing down their metabolism.

Light

For all the sunlight pouring down on the ocean's surface, none reaches the deep ocean bottom. Some light reflects off the surface; some is scattered or absorbed in sea water. Tiny bits of soil or other particles in sea water scatter light energy, changing its downward direction and sending light back toward the surface or off at an angle.

Absorption converts light energy into heat. The longest wavelengths of light (infrared) and the shortest wavelengths (ultraviolet) disappear in shallow sea water: they're absorbed in the first three feet of water. Red and purple light vanish 30 feet (9 meters) down. Blue-green light penetrates deepest; in very clear water, blue-green light may reach 600 feet (183 meters) deep.

Scientists use light penetration to describe different habitats in the open sea: the upper sunlit zone, the middle twilight zone and the deepest zone of darkness.

The photic or sunlit zone is the most active layer of the ocean. In this shallow region, storm waves, tides and currents keep the water in motion. Upwelling mixes in natural fertilizers from deeper waters. In central California, the photic zone can reach 300 feet

Deep sea squid

(91 meters) down. These waters are rich with life: microscopic plants called phytoplankton grow in this well-lit region, using light energy for photosynthesis. Planktonic animals like copepods, arrowworms and larval fishes are also abundant here, feeding on the plants or on the plant-eaters.

Below the sunlit region is a twilight zone of faint light. This midwater zone extends from about 300 feet to 3,500 feet (1,066 meters) below the surface. Many fishes like the bristlemouths found in the twilight zone are migrators that swim up each night to feed in the richer photic waters above and return to the depths each day.

The deepest zones never see the light of day. In the darkness below 3,500 feet (1,066 meters), the waters are cold and rich in nutrients, but without light, there is no plant production. Instead, the deepest organisms eat other deep sea animals or depend on other food raining down from shallower waters.

Adaptations in Deep Sea Animals

Look at all the seaweeds, invertebrates and fishes crowded together on our rocky shores. Compared to these complex communities in shallow water, deep sea animals are few and

Siphonophore

far between, forming patches of life in the seasonless depths. Most deep sea animals just don't look or act like their shallow-water cousins. The unusual body shapes and colors and behavior of deep sea animals may seem strange to us, but these adaptations suit them for survival in their deep, dark habitats.

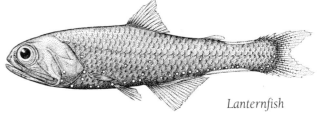

Lanternfish

Camouflage

In the darkness of the deep sea, an animal's body color can camouflage it or attract attention. Transparent midwater invertebrates like arrowworms seem invisible in the dim ocean twilight. Midwater fishes like the hatchetfish have silvery skin that reflects light. In the deeper dark habitats, fishes like gulper eels have black skin to help them hide in the darkness, while red shrimps and purple jellies appear black in the absence of red light.

Bioluminescence

Bioluminescence, the production of light by living animals, is a common adaptation in deep sea fishes and invertebrates. Some animals grow luminescent bacteria in special body pockets; others produce their own light in body organs called photophores. In the darkness of the deep sea, animals can use light to inform, confuse or attract other deep sea animals.

Some animals, like deep sea jellies and squid, use bioluminescence to escape danger. To distract predatory fishes, these escape artists release a bioluminescent substance and then swim away to safety in the darkness. Biological lights, like the

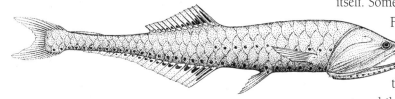

Bristlemouth

luminous "bait" on the top fin of the anglerfish, can also help lure prey. Photophores arranged in specific patterns help fishes like lanternfishes recognize potential mates. The lights may also work like taillights on a car to help a lanternfish judge its distance from other fish in a school.

Vision

Besides making their own light, many midwater animals have visual adaptations to the darkness. Fishes and invertebrates in the twilight zone have large, well-developed eyes. Some have eyes that are dark-adapted to see more red; others have optical lenses that can detect bioluminescence or concentrate the dim twilight. In contrast to the twilight zone, many animals in the darkest depths have small, poorly developed eyes.

Feeding

In the deep sea where food is scarce, animals have adapted to make the most of every meal. Compared to the sleek, muscular tuna of shallower water, a deep sea fish doesn't need as much food to support its small, flabby body, weak muscles and lightweight skeleton. A fish like the gulper eel with its huge mouth, unhinging jaws and expanding stomach can engulf and swallow a fish larger than itself. Some fishes migrate to areas with more food. Fishes like bristlemouths swim upward to feed in shallow water at night and return to hide in the depths during the day. Other fishes feed in shallow water while they're young, moving into deeper water as they mature.

Reproduction

How does a deep sea animal ever find a mate in the darkness? A fish with keen vision may focus on attractive lights and shapes; one with an acute sense of smell follows its nose. Incredibly different in size and shape, some male and female anglerfish have developed mating behavior that keeps them together for life. The tiny male anglerfish uses his keen sense of smell to search out the larger female and then bites on to permanently attach himself as a parasite on her. The parasitic male anglerfish relies on the female's circulatory system to nourish him. His sole remaining function is to produce sperm for reproduction.

Anglerfish

Scientists use submersibles like Deep Rover *to study the deep sea.*

Some animals like arrowworms have adapted in the opposite extreme, eliminating differences between the sexes by developing both male and female sexual organs. An hermaphrodite, an animal that is both male and female, can make both eggs and sperm. An animal that is only female must locate a male of the same species to reproduce; encounters with other females (half the population) won't be successful. In contrast, any two hermaphrodites can mate and when they do, twice as many eggs can be fertilized at one time. A hermaphrodite that can fertilize its own eggs has added insurance that it can reproduce even if it never finds a mate.

The strange-looking animals of the deep sea probably have many other adaptations that we don't yet understand. There's still a huge, mysterious world of animals deep below for us to explore.

Pressure in the Deep

Have you ever noticed how water pressure feels? The next time you go swimming, dive down to the bottom of the pool. Do you feel pressure in your ears? That's the pressure of the water pressing on your ear drums. Try some experiments to learn more about pressure.

MATERIALS
• Straw
• Cup of water

Where do you think it's hardest to blow through a straw: into the air, just below the surface of water or just above the bottom of a cup of water? Take a guess, then try blowing through the straw into the air and into different places in a cup of water. Where is it hardest to blow? (It's hardest to blow when the straw is near the cup's bottom.) Why is it hardest to blow there? (Pressure increases as you go deeper.)

More Pressure in the Deep

MATERIALS
• Two milk cartons: one half-gallon size and one quart size
• Pencil
• Tape
• Deep pan
• Water

Use the pencil to poke two identical holes in each milk carton: make one hole two inches from the bottom, the other hole three inches above the first. Stand one carton in a deep pan, tape the holes closed and fill the carton with water. Remove the two pieces of tape. As the water shoots out, how does the flow change? (It slows down because there's less pressure as the water drains out.) Which hole squirts farthest? Why? (The bottom hole squirts farther because there's more pressure the deeper you go.) Fill the second carton with water to the same depth as the first and repeat the experiment to show that depth, not volume, causes greater pressure.

Even More Pressure in the Deep

MATERIALS
• Plastic garbage
bag
• Deep container
(A plastic water pail
works great!)

Do you think pressure comes from above, below or all around? To test your guess, put your arm and hand in a plastic garbage bag and immerse them in a deep container of water. Where do you feel pressure? (The pressure comes from all sides.) Animals in the deep sea live in pressure that is a hundred times greater than we live in on land.

How do these animals survive such forces? (Hint: only the gas spaces in animals' bodies are crushed by pressure. Water and most oils don't compress under pressure.)

Changing Colors

MATERIALS

- Blue, green, red and yellow sheets of colored plastic
- Hole punch
- Red, blue, green, yellow and black construction paper (one sheet of each color)
- One yard of black material
- Graph paper
- Pencil

Do this one by yourself, at school or at a party!

Experience the color changes that occur 100 feet (30 meters) under water. Look at objects of various colors through filters made of colored plastic. Which colors disappear in blue light? What happens to the objects when you look through a red or dark green filter? What happens to the colors? Why does this happen? (Read about light in the section, "What Is the Deep Sea?" on page 90.) In the deep sea, blue-green light penetrates the deepest; all other colors are absorbed in shallower water. Deep sea animals, like many animals, often have coloration to help camouflage them. Experiment with the blue-colored plastic. What colors would best help deep sea animals blend in with their surroundings? (The color red looks black in the deep sea.) If you look at deep sea animals, many are red and black!

Searching for prey

Using a hole punch, make five sets of colored dots (20 each in blue, red, yellow, green and black). Scatter all the dots on a square yard of black material and take turns as predators. Each predator gets 15 seconds to pick up dots, one at a time. How many dots did each predator collect? Make a bar graph comparing the color and number of dots collected by each predator. Which color dot was captured most often? Would predators be more efficient if all prey were black? Would predators be more efficient if they worked together as a team?

Try the above activity again, but this time look through blue filters when picking up the colored dots. Compare your results. How do these results relate to prey colors in the deep sea?

Design an Animal

MATERIALS
- Paper
- Favorite drawing materials

Design and draw animals suited to live in a cold, dark environment under great pressure. What adaptations help your animals cope with the physical conditions of the deep sea? How do they find food, avoid being eaten, reproduce and communicate with one another?

What Do You Think?

MATERIALS
- Paper
- Pencil

Nuclear wastes, dredge spoils, sewage treatment plant effluents and other wastes are sometimes dumped in the deep sea. Research and discuss these issues with your friends, classmates or family. Draft a management plan for one of these issues, then poll others about different management options. Build the results of your polls into your plan as appropriate, then share your findings with people who play a key role in making decisions (for instance, elected officials and people holding key positions in appropriate organizations).

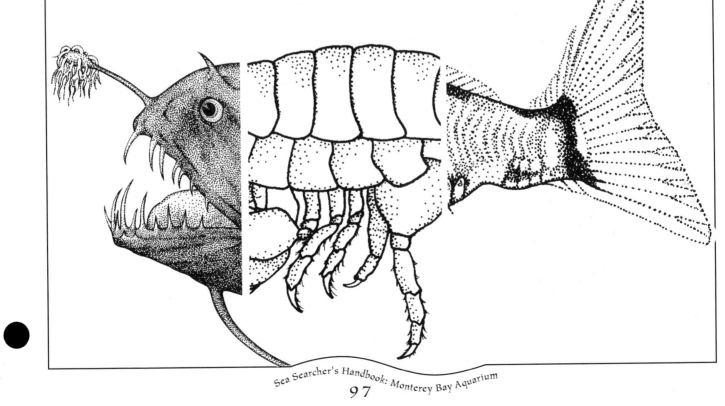

What's It like Down There?

MATERIALS
- A variety of arts and crafts materials

Exploring the deep sea is much like exploring your town from a blimp during the night and taking samples with a butterfly net attached to a long string. How long would it take to get a complete picture of the environment you're studying? Would you ever? Invent and build models of equipment that would help you better study the deep sea. Debate the costs, risks and benefits of using a remotely-operated vehicle (ROV) versus actually being there.

Unknown Worlds

MATERIALS
- Paper
- Pen or pencil

List several ways the deep sea is similar to and different from outer space. Would you like to explore these environments? What would you hope to find? What would you bring on an expedition to outer space? What would you bring to explore the deep sea? Are these kinds of explorations worthwhile things to do? Why? How do you feel about going to an unknown place? Record your thoughts on a piece of paper. Share them with your family or friends.

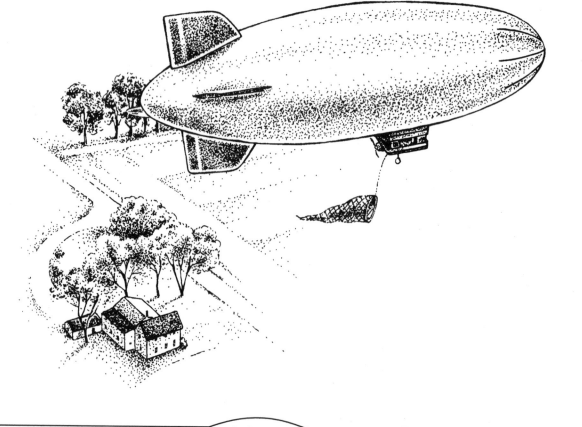

Schooling Fishsticks

A great activity for a party!

Each species of deep sea lanternfish glows with a unique pattern of body lights. These lights, called photophores, help lanternfishes find mates and avoid predators in the darkness of the deep sea. Photophores along the side of a fish's body attract mates, while those on its belly help the fish match the dim light above, protecting it from predators. Bioluminescent light may help other fishes form schools to avoid or confuse predators.

MATERIALS
- One 18" stick or dowel for each student
- Cardboard for mounting fish patterns
- One copy of the lanternfish pattern (both sides) for each student
- Black permanent marker
- Tape
- Glue
- Optional: Non-toxic glow-in-the-dark paints (available at arts and crafts supply stores)
- Brushes

Getting started

Make a copy of the lanternfish pattern (both sides) for each child. Cut out the pattern. Glue one half of the fish pattern to one side of the cardboard and the other half to the other side of the cardboard to form a sturdy lanternfish. Trim the cardboard to match the fish's shape. Divide the paper fishes into groups (four or five fish per group). Give each fish group a unique pattern of lights: use the marker to darken specific spots on each fish in a group. (The light patterns on both sides of a fish should match. Each group has a different pattern, but fish in the same group have the same pattern to show they're the same species.) You can paint the light spots with glow-in-the-dark paint to represent bioluminescent spots. Attach the fishes to the sticks with tape.

Getting ready

Make a copy of this lanternfish pattern (both sides) for each child. For a BIG impact, enlarge the fish on a copy machine.

Lights attract attention

Mix up all of the fishsticks, then give one to each child and ask: Where do you think lanternfishes live? What clues helped you guess where they live? Why do you think they're called lanternfishes? Explain that each species of lanternfish has a unique pattern of body lights to help them find mates. Have children hold their fishsticks up to attract the attention of other fish with the same light pattern. Look-alikes unite into their groups. (If you've painted glow-in-the-dark spots on the fishes, turn out the lights for this part of the activity.) Have each group of children list ideas about how bioluminescence helps lanternfishes survive.

Schooling for survival

You can use the fishsticks to show children how schooling fishes move. (Lanternfishes don't school, but you can use them as an example.) Outside, let each group of children swim a simple course, following these rules:

The fish swim close together, but without touching.

All fish in a school maintain the same speed and direction.

The front fish of the school determines the direction and speed for all.

Each time the school turns, the front fish becomes the new leader.

A school that is forced to divide must reunite as soon as possible.

How did you feel about being part of a school? What was difficult about moving as a group? What was easy? What cues did you use to stay together? Would it be harder to school in the dark? Why? How does schooling help fishes?

To show how fishes school to survive, you can have many species unite to form a huge school, using the same rules. Have the school swim a fixed course while you play the predator. Attack the school, but only capture those fishes that leave the ranks. The school may change direction to avoid you, but it must stick to the course. (No running.) If a fish turns or changes speed to avoid a predator, the rest of the school must follow. A fish who's caught becomes a predator and may help attack the school. The game ends when the school reaches the end of the course or when all the children have been captured.

How did being in a large school differ from being in a small school? Did you feel safer from predators at the outer edge or in the middle of the school? If predators formed a school, do you think they would find food more effectively? Why or why not?

Follow-up

Grow bioluminescent bacteria at home or in your classroom. To grow the bacteria, you'll need luminescent bacteria (*Vibrio fischeri*) plates and photobacterium agar plates. You can order these from: Carolina Biological Supply Company, P.O. Box 187, Gladstone, Oregon, 97027. Instructions are included.

Visit an aquarium to observe schools of fishes. Do real fishes follow the same rules for schooling? What land animals work together in groups? How are they different from schools of fishes?

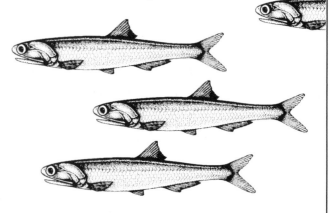

School of anchovies

Gulper eel
Eurypharynx pelecanoides
SIZE: TO 16 IN. (40 CM)

The gulper eel's species name, *pelecanoides*, comes from its pouchlike mouth that looks like a pelican's bill. This fish usually eats prawns and small fishes, but with its huge mouth, it may swallow even larger prey. When hungry, this flexible fish may wriggle its tail in front of its mouth. The tail's tip glows in the dark and may lure prey close.

Deep sea squid
Histioteuthis meleagroteuthis SIZE: TO 12 IN. (30 CM)

All squids, from this foot-long deep sea species to its 50-foot-long relative, grab prey with their two longest tentacles. And all squids use their eight arms to carry prey to their mouths. But unlike other squids, the deep sea squid's left eye is much larger than its right one. Each eye works differently, but no one's sure why. How do you think the different-sized eyes might help this animal survive?

Filetail catshark
Parmaturus xaniurus SIZE: TO 22 IN. (56 CM)

A filetail catshark swims gracefully along the muddy seafloor. Gray-brown above and pale below, this fish blends in with its benthic habitat. Its large green eyes look upward, unlike those of shallow-water sharks. Catsharks lay eggs with curly corners. The curls catch on edges of rocks and sponges to anchor the egg case near the deep seafloor. Here it'll stay for two years while a tiny catshark grows inside.

Siphonophore

Apolemia sp. SIZE: TO 98 FT. (30 M)

A siphonophore is a chain of specialized parts, each one plays a role in the life of this animal. A floating buoy leads, followed by a cluster of round swimming bells that pulse to propel the chain (which can stretch nearly half the length of a football field). To eat, a siphonophore dangles a curtain of stinging tentacles that stun shrimp, jellies and other prey. The tentacles carry the prey to one of the mouth parts.

Blackdragon

Idiacanthus antrostomus SIZE: TO 15 IN. (38 CM)

How can you tell a female blackdragon from a male? A female is darker and larger, and a long whiskerlike barbel dangles from her chin. At night, she swims hundreds of feet up to the sea's surface to feed. At dawn, she makes her way back down to the deep sea. Without a working stomach, a male doesn't migrate for food. Unable to eat, he may only live for a year, just long enough to mate.

Shining tubeshoulder

Sagamichthys abei SIZE: TO 13 IN. (33 CM)

Tiny tubelike projections above each pectoral fin set this fish apart from others. Tubeshoulders can squirt a bioluminescent cloud from their tubes, perhaps dazzling predators with a flash of light as they slip away into the darkness. Tubeshoulders, born with gray-blue bodies and white tails, become shiny black as adults. As they grow, photophores develop along their undersides and on their heads.

Deep sea shrimp

Sergestes similis SIZE: TO 1.5 IN. (4 CM)

This shrimp's long antennae—nearly four times the length of its body—may help this animal find food or mates by sensing chemicals produced by other animals. This shrimp also uses bioluminescence to help it survive. Light-producing organs dot the underside of its red-and-white splotched body. The lights may attract mates, or they may help the shrimp hide from hungry predators.

Hatchetfish

Argyropelecus sp. SIZE: TO 4 IN. (10 CM)

Shaped like the head of a tiny hatchet, this fish is countershaded to hide it from predators. Its back is dark; its belly is shiny silver with two rows of glowing photophores. A hatchetfish scans the water above for prey with tubular eyes. Its eyes can focus near or far, but only upward. Its large mouth points upward, too, ready to snap up prey once it's been seen.

Amphipod

Cystisoma fabricii SIZE: TO 6 IN. (15 CM)

This amphipod swims slowly through the water, paddling its three pairs of swimming legs located near the rear of its body. Swimming slowly may be fine; its crystal clear body probably makes it hard for predators to see in the dim light. This crustacean's two huge compound eyes may help it to scan the dimly lit water in search of prey, though scientists don't know yet what it eats.

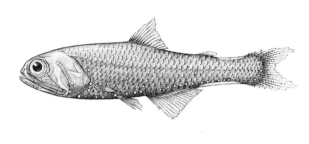

Lanternfish

Stenobrachius leucopsarus SIZE: TO 5 IN. (13 CM)
Each species of lanternfish has its own pattern of light-producing photophores. Lanternfishes may use these patterns to find mates of their own species. Some males may attract mates by flashing a large photophore near their tails. Or maybe this light confuses predators, causing them to attack the male's bright tail instead of his darker head. What do you think the lanternfish uses its taillights for?

Anglerfish

Linophryne coronata SIZE: TO 4 IN. (10 CM)
A female anglerfish may attract prey with lights: part of her top fin looks like a fishing pole with bait that lights up. The glowing bait may lure fishes to her huge mouth. A male, barely half the female's size, depends on a female for food. Once mature, he may use his keen sense of smell to find a mate. Then he bites her and hangs on. His body fuses to hers and they become mates for life.

Bristlemouth

Cyclothone sp. SIZE: TO 3 IN. (8 CM)
Many species of bristlemouths live below 1,000 feet (300 meters) where there's little light. Like many deep sea fishes, some of these bristlemouth species have poorly developed eyes and must rely on other senses to make their way in the darkness.

"If happiness consists in the number of pleasing emotions that occupy our mind—how true it is that the contemplation of nature, which always gives rise to these emotions, is one of the great sources of happiness."

THOMAS BELT (1832-1878)
INTRODUCTION TO *THE NATURALIST IN NICARAGUA*

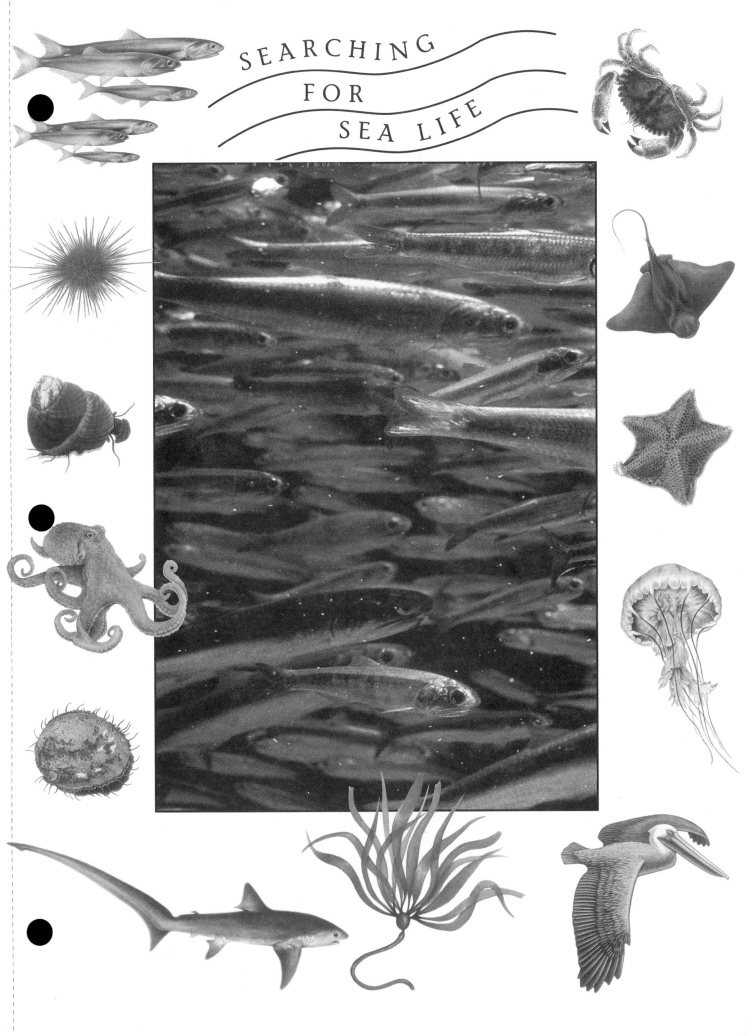

Searching For Sea Life

Suited for the Sea

Strategies for Survival

Plants and animals have special body parts, shapes and behaviors that help them survive in their habitats. From paddlelike feet that burrow in the sand to graceful tentacles that stun prey, each adaptation is unique in the way that it helps a creature cope with its surroundings and live a particular lifestyle.

Because every habitat has its own special character and living conditions, the creatures in each must be specially adapted to live there. Deep sea fishes, living in a world of darkness, blink lights to attract food and mates. At the rocky shore where waves batter the rocks, adaptations like a barnacle's feathery feet let some animals strain food from the water while they hold on tight. Some adaptations seem unbelievable: a young flatfish (larva) swims through the water, one eye on each side of its head, like a typical fish. But an adult flatfish lives on the seafloor and has both eyes on the same side of its head. The adult's body is flattened side to side (unlike a bat ray's that's flattened top to bottom) and it always lies on one side of its body. As the young flatfish grows, its body gets flatter and one eye migrates to join the other on the upward-facing side of its head.

On land or in the sea, plants and animals face the same challenges: they must find nutrients, protect

Gulper eel

themselves and reproduce in order to survive. You can learn about a plant or animal's adaptive features by taking note of its living conditions and looking for ways its behavior, body parts and shape help it survive those conditions.

Feeding strategies

An animal's adaptations to find, catch and eat prey depend on what and where the animal eats. Some animals chase their prey; most open sea fishes (like tuna, salmon and some sharks), with their strong, sleek bodies, can swim faster over greater distances than herring, squid and other prey.

Other animals, like barnacles and mussels, spend their adult lives attached to one spot. Not able to chase their prey, these animals filter tiny drifting plants and animals from the water.

In the deep sea where food is scarce, some fishes have special adaptations to lure prey: the anglerfish's dorsal fin dangles in front of its large mouth like a fishing line with bait. Some plant eaters, like the turban snail and most chiton, use a radula (a filelike tongue) to rasp kelp and other algae.

Sometimes one animal's feeding needs benefit another animal. A fish like the señorita has small, protruding teeth to pick parasites off other fishes.

Protection

For a plant or animal to survive, it must avoid being eaten by predators and cope with its habitat's physical conditions. Sometimes the same adaptations that protect an animal from its living conditions also protect it from predators.

On the wave-battered rocky shore, animals have body parts and shapes that help them hold on, lie flat, bend with the waves or hide. A snail or a chiton has a strong, muscular foot to hold on tight; sea stars have thousands of tiny tube feet with suction-cup ends. The Chinese-hat shape of limpets and barnacles and the flat shape of chitons and abalone offer little resistance to the water rushing past. Flexible seaweeds bend rather than break, and a crab's flattened shell lets it crawl into narrow rock crevices.

Sea anemone

The sandy seafloor's shifting sand offers nothing firm for plants and animals to hang on to, so large sea plants and sessile (attached) animals can't live here. With nothing to hide behind, most animals, like olive snails and some anemones, escape predators by burrowing in the sand.

Other sandy seafloor animals, like sanddabs and halibut, change color and pattern to match their speckled brown-and-white surroundings. Most open sea fishes have camouflaged coloration, too. Light on their bellies and dark on top, they blend in with the darker depths below and the light streaming in from above.

Halibut

Behavioral adaptations also protect animals from predators and harsh living conditions. A decorator crab plants a garden of seaweeds, sponges and other sessile plants and animals on its back to escape detection. On the rocky shore where low tide leaves some animals exposed, mussels and barnacles close their shells tightly, trapping water inside to avoid drying out.

Reproduction

Though an animal may successfully find food and protect itself, it must also reproduce to keep its population healthy. To find mates, animals display an array of colors, shapes, lights, smells and behaviors. Adaptations for reproduction are just as diverse. Most invertebrates (like sea urchins and chitons) and most fishes broadcast thousands of eggs and sperm to drift in the sea's current, but only a few will survive to reproduce. Some fishes, like the lingcod, guard a nest of eggs on the seafloor, while others, like the surfperch and some sharks, give birth to live young. Marine mammals bear and nurse one or two live young, like we do.

Decorator crab

Next time you're on a walk or at an aquarium, take a look at the plants and animals around you. How do they find and catch food? How do they protect themselves from being eaten? The plants and animals we see are the ones that can survive their habitat's conditions, reproduce and pass their adaptations on to future generations.

At Home in the Sea

MATERIALS
• Paper
• Pencil
• Magazines
• Glue

On a piece of paper, draw a line down the middle from top to bottom, dividing it in half. Pick an animal from the sea. On the left side, make a list of all the basic things your animal needs to survive. On the right side, make a list of the things you need to survive. How are your lists the same? How are they different?

On the back of the paper, draw a picture of your animal. What body parts help it get the things it needs to survive? What behaviors help it survive?

Draw pictures of your home, including what you need to live (water, food and a place to sleep). Cut out a magazine picture of a sea animal, then glue the picture on a blank piece of paper and draw in the animal's home around it. How do the animal's body parts and behaviors help it survive in its home?

Animal needs for Survival

Food
Home
Water
Protection

I need for survival

Home
Food
Clothes
Money

A Book about Sea Life

MATERIALS
•Paper
• Your favorite
drawing materials

Make a book about sea life. Show how plants and animals of the sea are adapted to their homes. How do seaweeds along the shore survive crashing waves? How do animals move? How do they breathe? How do they eat and protect themselves?

Clothes That Hide

MATERIALS
• Clothes

Plan a Camouflage Day. Choose a habitat, either on land or in the sea, and wear clothes that would camouflage you in that habitat.

You may want to choose a sea habitat one day and a land habitat another day to compare. What behaviors would help you hide?

A blue cape, hat, and a pair of flippers provide camouflage in the open sea.

An outfit of green ribbons with a green cape would be difficult to spot in a bed of eelgrass.

Hide and Seek

A great activity to do
at a party or at school!

MATERIALS
• Cutouts of blank
paper birds—one for
each child
• Crayons or other
drawing materials

Give each child a blank paper bird. Divide the group of children into two equal parts and let each half explore a 10-by-10-foot area outside. (To make the game more exciting, choose areas with different kinds of vegetation.) Have the children pick places to hide their birds, then have them color their birds to blend in with their hiding spots. Now the children are ready to hide their birds. Explain that the birds should be hidden in plain sight, not covered up.

When all the birds are hidden, have each team try to find the other team's birds. Discuss which birds were hardest to find, which were easiest and why. Pick up the paper birds for the children to take home and hang on their walls.

Suited for Survival

MATERIALS
- Paper
- Drawing materials
- Clothes, fabric, scarves and other wearable items

Pick a habitat (like the rocky shore, kelp forest or sandy seafloor) that you'd like to live in for two weeks. Design, draw and construct a survival suit that includes adaptations for feeding, moving, hiding and protecting yourself.

With a mop for disguise, this kelp forest animal strains plankton from the sea.

A flashlight blinks on and off in the deep sea—perhaps to attract prey.

A plunger helps this rocky shore animal hold on tight when waves crash.

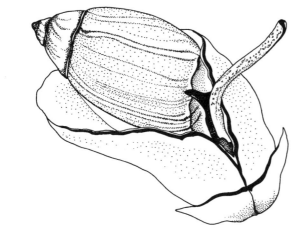

Olive snail

Olivella biplicata SIZE: TO 1 IN. (2.5 CM)

The olive snail plows through the sand just below the surface, leaving a furrow behind. Its smooth, streamlined shell helps it slip through the sand. To breathe, the snail sends a tube above the sand. The olive snail eats dead animals and plants. It may also gather tiny food bits from the sand.

California halibut

Paralichthys californicus SIZE: TO 5 FT. (1.5 M)

A halibut has both eyes on the same side of its head. It lives on the sandy seafloor, always lying on one side of its body. The halibut wriggles its flat body into the sand; its two eyes stick out above the sand to watch for approaching predators and prey.

Hermit crab

Pagurus samuelis SIZE: TO 1 IN. (2.5 CM)

A hermit crab wears an empty snail shell to protect its soft body. The back legs hold the shell on tight. As the crab grows, it needs bigger shells. One hermit crab will even steal a good shell from another crab. Though a hermit crab threatens and fights with its large claws, it's not a hunter. This crab eats seaweeds and dead animals.

Purple sea urchin
Strongylocentrotus purpuratus
SIZE: TO 4 IN. (10 CM)

Using their spines and teeth, urchins burrow slowly into solid rock. Because they grow as they dig, some end up trapped in holes, too big to leave. Between the hard spines, an urchin has hundreds of tube feet. Its soft tube feet are always busy: some hold the urchin onto the rock; others move kelp to the urchin's greedy mouth.

Sea anemone
Anthopleura elegantissima SIZE: TO 10 IN. (25 CM)

The sea anemone looks like a flower on a thick, bumpy stalk, but it's really an animal. The flowery parts are tentacles with stingers. The stingers zap small animals that get too close; then the anemone swallows them whole. At low tide, the anemone closes up. Bits of shell stuck to the bumpy flesh help keep the sea anemone from drying out.

Ochre star
Pisaster ochraceus SIZE: TO 1 FT. (30 CM)

This sea star has hundreds of tiny suction-cup feet under each arm that help it stick to rocks. The sea star is a real loafer; it clings motionless to a rock for weeks. Even a hungry sea star isn't hasty. Slow and steady, its feet can pry apart a mussel. When the mussel's two shells open, the sea star slides its stomach between the shells to digest the animal inside.

Marine Mammals

Orca chasing salmon

What Is a Marine Mammal?

Cold and dark as the sea is, some mammals have adapted to life there. Mammals that live in the ocean range in size from the furry, five-foot-long sea otter to the enormous blue whale, a hundred feet long. What do these creatures have in common? Like us, they are warm-blooded animals that breathe air, have hair and nurse their young.

More than 30 species of marine mammals live in or pass through Monterey Bay. Three major groups of marine mammals can be seen here: cetaceans (whales, dolphins and porpoises), pinnipeds (seals and sea lions) and sea otters. Each group evolved from different land mammals that moved back to the sea.

The cetaceans descended from a cowlike ancestor that returned to ocean life about 65 million years ago. The streamlined, fishlike whale doesn't resemble its four-legged ancestor. With one or two nostrils on the top of its head, a whale can easily breathe at the surface without lifting its head. Its tail is incredibly strong, forceful enough to push the whale through the water. But tiny leg bones deep in the whale's body and handlike bones inside its flippers remind us of its land-dwelling ancestors.

The pinnipeds are graceful and agile swimmers with smooth, tapering bodies and strong flippers, but they still retain many ties to land. Most return to shore to mate and give birth, some more gracefully than others. "Eared" seals, like the California sea lion, have small external ears and versatile hind flippers they can turn under to "walk" on land. They evolved from bearlike mammals that returned to the sea about 30 million years ago. "Earless" seals, like the harbor seal, evolved from otterlike ancestors about 14 million years ago. These true seals don't have visible ears or walking flippers; on land, they wriggle awkwardly on their bellies.

The sea otter, adapted to living in the ocean over the past four million years, still resembles the weasel, its relative on land.

Gray whale skeleton

Sea otters live close to shore; they're not as well equipped for the open ocean as the streamlined, deep-diving seals and whales.

Feeding

The largest marine mammals eat the smallest food. Baleen whales, like the humpback and blue whales, strain millions of small, shrimplike crustaceans from the water with their sievelike baleen.

Baleen plates hang in rows from the whale's upper jaw. The baleen fibers, made of the same material as fingernails and claws, fray toward the inside of the mouth and overlap to form a dense net. The whale swallows a great mouthful of food and water, then closes its jaws. With a thrust of its tongue, it expels the water through the baleen, leaving the prey trapped inside. The gray whale feeds on muddy bottoms, straining amphipod crustaceans from the sediments with its shorter, stubby baleen.

Toothed marine mammals use their teeth to grasp, rip or crush fishes and squids. With their strong jaws and doglike teeth, seals and sea lions tear at their prey. Dolphins and toothed whales make clicking sounds and use the echoes to find (echolocate) and possibly to stun their prey. With peglike teeth, these cetaceans grip a fish and swallow it whole. Although many whales and seals are solitary feeders, orcas often feed in a group called a pod. Hunting together like a pack of wolves, a pod of orcas can surround a school of salmon or even overwhelm a larger whale.

Sea otters keep to shallow waters, eating whatever is readily available in kelp forests. They hunt while they dive, collecting crabs, clams and other shellfish with their agile front paws. Afloat on the surface, they use rock tools to smash the shells. With strong canine teeth for prying and powerful molars for crushing, sea otters break open and devour their prey.

Keeping warm

How do marine mammals generate enough body heat to keep warm in the cold ocean?

Their large appetites and fast digestion fuel the high metabolic rates that produce body heat. Other adaptations help maintain that heat in a marine mammal's body.

A whale has a thick, insulating layer of fat called blubber to help retain body heat. The layer of blubber also makes the whale buoyant and supplies energy when food is scarce. Seals have both a blubber layer and a coat of hair for insulation. Of all the

California sea lion

marine mammals, only sea otters lack blubber, depending instead on insulation from their dense fur coats. An otter must groom and clean itself constantly to keep the fur waterproof.

A whale also has a special circulatory system that helps maintain its core body temperature. In an overheated animal, the outer blood vessels dilate to allow warm blood to flow out to cooler fins and flippers. In a chilled animal, the outer blood vessels constrict to reduce blood flow to the extremities. Cool blood flowing from the outer body back to the heart recaptures heat from warm blood flowing away from the heart in a counter-current heat exchange.

Migrator or resident, a marine mammal spends a lot of time under water holding its breath. Sperm whales are the deepest divers, known to dive for an hour or more to at least 3,700 feet (1,100 meters). To prolong its underwater time, the animal's metabolism and heartbeat slow down and its lungs collapse. Because they breathe air, marine mammals must return to the surface at regular intervals.

Communication

On land, seals and sea lions communicate with barks and bellows. Some whales (like humpbacks) sing beautifully under water.

Sei whale

Migration and locomotion

Most marine mammals are social creatures. They may swim together, rubbing and playing in groups of two, three or more. Some, like sea otters and some pinnipeds, reside in coastal areas. Others, like baleen whales, are world travelers. Each year, baleen whales migrate between their polar feeding areas and the tropical areas where they breed and give birth. Passing Monterey Bay twice a year, the gray whales swim more than 10,000 miles (16,000 kilometers) from the Bering Sea to Baja California and back, the longest migration known of any mammal.

Blue whales call long distance with bursts of low-frequency sound (below the range of human hearing). Such sounds may travel hundreds of miles under water.

Others, like orcas, communicate with clicks. Each orca pod has its own dialect, its own catalog of clicks and squeaks. Neighboring pods share some calls; the more the pods interact, the more their dialects will overlap. Toothed whales and dolphins also use sound as a kind of sonar echolocation—to find out about objects they can't see. Sperm whales may even use blasts of sound to stun their prey.

Only otters and eared seals like sea lions have external ears. True seals and whales have hidden ears but they still can hear.

People and marine mammals

For thousands of years, people hunted marine mammals for food, oil, clothing and tools.

In Monterey Bay, whalers hunted mostly humpbacks and gray whales between 1854 and 1925. Long ago, when the shore whalers used small boats and limited weapons, whales had a fair chance of surviving. But

with advancing technology, some whales were hunted nearly to extinction: humpbacks, blue whales, gray whales, sperm whales, elephant seals and sea otters.

Scientists and conservationists brought the plight of the marine mammals to public attention. As people have learned more about the lives of marine mammals, they have grown to respect and value them as an integral part of the ocean environment. Marine mammals are now protected by the Marine Mammal Protection Act in the United States. Since 1972, it's been illegal to kill or harass marine mammals or collect their bones, fur or other parts.

Now, scientists study marine mammals to learn how they interact with each other and with their environment. Researchers track them with radio tags and satellites, identify them individually with photographs, listen to them with underwater microphones and observe their group behavior. Such research has shown that these benign and probably intelligent animals form complex social groups and communicate with one another.

Humpback whale

For many marine mammals, the future is still uncertain. With continued protection and research, perhaps these warm-blooded animals will find safety in their ocean home.

PRIMARY SUMMER
FEEDING AREA
June-October

Bering Sea

Chukchi Sea

Unimak
Pass

Beaufort Sea

Alaska, U.S.

Gulf of Alaska

Canada

Pacific Ocean

Vancouver Island

Newport, Oregon

San Francisco
Monterey

San Diego

PRIMARY WINTER
MATING AND
CALVING AREA
January-April

Mexico

Guerrero Negro
Lagoon

Baja
California

Scammon's Lagoon

San Ignacio Lagoon

Magdalena Lagoon

*Annual migration route
of gray whales*

What Is a Gray Whale?

During winter, the baleen whale you'd most likely see along North America's Pacific Coast is the gray whale. The adult gray whale is a medium-sized whale, 36 to 50 feet (11 to 15 meters) in length (a little longer than a school bus) and weighing 20 to 45 tons (18 to 41 metric tons). Every winter, thousands of gray whales migrate south from their cold-water summer feeding grounds in the Arctic seas to the warm-water lagoons of western Baja California in Mexico. This journey is more than 10,000 miles (16,000 kilometers) round trip, the longest of all known mammal migrations.

Feeding and diet

Gray whales do most of their feeding from May to November in the cold northern seas. Unlike other baleen whales that filter food from the water, the gray whale usually eats from the bottom. Rolling on its side (usually the right side), the whale sucks up a mouthful of mud or sand. With a thrust of its tongue, the whale expels the mud through baleen plates that hang from its upper jaw. The baleen acts like a strainer, filtering shrimplike amphipods and other prey from the mud.

The gray whales gorge themselves during these months, eating about 1,000 pounds (455 kilograms) of food a day and gaining six to 12 inches (15 to 30 centimeters) of body fat. This fat provides the primary source of energy for the trip from the Arctic to Baja California and back. For a pregnant whale, these fat reserves not only get her to Mexico, but provide fuel for her and her calf on the return trip.

Baleen

Migration

In October, when the days begin to shorten and ice starts to form on the Bering Sea, pregnant females begin their migration south. They are soon followed by nonpregnant females, mature males and juveniles. Most of the 21,000 gray whales that live in the eastern Pacific migrate to the Mexican lagoons every year, passing through Monterey Bay from late November to mid-February.

Gray whales travel close to shore in small groups (pods) of two to 15 whales. The trip each way takes eight to 10 weeks. Males and nonpregnant mature females court and mate throughout the southward journey. If you see two or three gray whales thrashing and splashing about in the water, they are probably courting and possibly mating.

Reproduction

Most pregnant females give birth when they reach the warmer Mexican waters, usually in January and February. Some have their calves during their migration south. A female gray whale is pregnant for about 13 months and gives birth to a one-ton calf every other year.

The whales' migration is timed so that the calves are born in warm water where they grow rapidly on their mother's rich milk. Gray whale milk is about 53 percent fat (compared to cow's milk which is 3.5 percent fat). A gray whale calf can gain 50 to 70 pounds (23 to 32 kilograms) a day. Calves are about 15 feet (five meters) long at birth, growing to 20 feet (six meters) long by the time they pass Monterey on the northward journey with their mothers. They are weaned at seven to nine months, reach maturity between five and 11 years and can live to be 50 years old.

During their time in the Mexican lagoons, the other adults continue courting and mating. In February and March, newly impregnated females begin the return trip north. Mature males leave first, followed by juveniles. Females with new calves are the last to leave the lagoons. You can see the whales heading north past Monterey from mid-February to mid-May.

Communication

Gray whales don't sing like humpback whales or click and whistle like dolphins, but they do make grunting sounds to communicate with one another. However, scientists aren't sure what the sounds mean or how these whales use them.

Like most whales, gray whales breach, rocketing nearly out of the water and falling back with a thunderous splash. Breaching and the slapping of flippers and flukes (tail fins) on the water may be forms of communication. Gray whales may also communicate by touch, especially females who often touch their calves.

Gray whales and people

Whether you watch gray whales from the shore or a boat, your first glimpse is usually its heart-shaped "blow" of misty vapor as it exhales at the surface. Look toward the horizon for the blow. A whale blows three to five times in a row, 10 to 20 seconds apart, before lifting its flukes out of the water as it starts, a three- to seven-minute dive. Sometimes you may see its mottled gray body with a row of six to 12 bumps, or knuckles, along the midline of its back. (Unlike many whales, the gray whale has no dorsal fin on its back.)

You can also recognize a gray whale by its parasites—the large whitish patches of barnacles attached to the skin. The barnacles don't harm the whale, they're just hitching a ride. Tan patches on the whale are large clusters of parasitic whale lice, amphipods that feed on the skin of the whale.

Over the years, people have had more of an interest in gray whales than just watching and studying them. Whalers made a living hunting them: first to make oil from their blubber (to light lamps and lubricate machinery), then later to make fertilizer from their meat and bone meal. Gray whales were easy to spot as they swam close to shore, and profits from whaling soared. Whaling stations popped up along the migration route—the central coast of California at Point Lobos, Moss Landing and MacAbee Beach. With the discovery of the Mexican breeding lagoons in 1855, even greater numbers were hunted. By the 1880s, the gray whale population had plummeted to near-extinction.

With fewer whales, profits fell. The gray whale population started to recover, until the next period of whaling occurred in the early 1900s. The introduction of floating factories and diesel-powered boats made hunting whales easier and more profitable.

Since the 1940s the gray whale population has been protected as an endangered species. The International Whaling Commission allows only Alaskan Eskimos and Soviet natives to harvest these whales for necessary food and supplies each year. Some scientists believe there may be as many gray whales now as there were before commercial whaling began.

Today, gray whales still deserve our protection. Pollution, boat traffic, industrial noise, offshore oil and natural gas exploration, fishing, whale watching and loss of habitat and food resources pose potential threats to these magnificent creatures of the sea. It's up to us to help protect them.

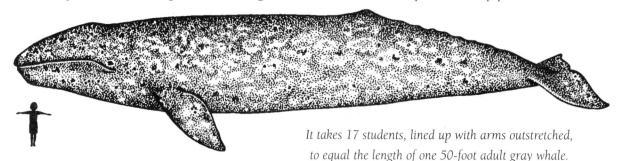

It takes 17 students, lined up with arms outstretched, to equal the length of one 50-foot adult gray whale.

What Is a Sea Otter

If you look out into a kelp bed off the central California coast and see what looks like a floating brown log, you may have spotted a sea otter. A closer look would show a long, dark-brown, furry animal with stubby front paws, large, webbed hind flippers and a whiskered face.

Sea otters are the smallest marine mammals in North America. (Only the marine otter—an endangered species that lives off the coast of South America—is smaller.) An average adult California sea otter is about the size of a ten-year-old child— four feet (1.2 meters) long. Females weigh about 44 pounds (20 kilograms), males about 64 pounds (29 kilograms).

Keeping warm

Sea otters live in 30° to 60° F (0° to 15° C) sea water, yet they maintain a constant internal body temperature of about 100° F (38° C). To keep warm they depend on their thick, water-resistant fur. Most other marine mammals have an insulating layer of fat, called blubber, to keep out the cold.

When you see a sea otter rubbing its body and rolling in the water, it's grooming its fur to keep it clean and waterproof. Depending on which part of a sea otter's body you look at, a square inch (6.5 square centimeters) of fur contains between 170,000 and one million hairs. (You have only about 100,000 hairs on your entire head.) As an otter grooms, it's coating each hair with natural oils from its skin and trapping tiny air bubbles in its fur.

The trapped air and oils make the fur water resistant and insulate the otter from the cold ocean water. If the fur becomes soiled, perhaps from oil or boat fuel, it gets matted, which destroys the protective bubble barrier. A soiled sea otter dies of exposure to the cold in just a few hours.

A sea otter cracks open an urchin while floating on its back in a kelp forest.

Sea otters also keep warm by burning calories from their food. A sea otter's metabolism (rate of heat production) is two to three times faster than similar-sized land mammals. Depending on the caloric content of its prey, an otter fuels its high metabolism by eating about 25 percent of its body weight in food every day. A 50-pound (23-kilogram) otter eats about 13 pounds (six kilograms) of seafood daily.

Habitat and locomotion

Sea otters live in the coastal waters of the northern Pacific Ocean from the Kuril Islands in Russia to Prince William Sound in Alaska. Smaller populations of sea otters live off the coasts of British Columbia, Washington State and California. In California, sea otters live along a 250-mile stretch of coast from Point Año Nuevo in Santa Cruz County south to Purisima Point in Santa Barbara County.

California sea otters live close to shore, usually in or near kelp forests. They rest in the kelp, often wrapping themselves in kelp fronds. Some otters spend time along sandy beaches and in harbors and sloughs. Unlike Alaskan otters, California sea otters seldom come ashore. When they do, they usually haul out on low, algae-covered rocks along the water's edge.

Ochre star and abalone

An otter swims on its back at the surface, pumping its hind flippers in unison. But when it's in a hurry, an otter will swim on its stomach. Some otters, usually females, stay within a few miles of where they were born. Males tend to travel farther, often exploring new areas.

Feeding and diet

There are more than 50 kinds of marine invertebrates on a sea otter's menu, including mussels, clams, abalone and other snails, octopuses, crabs, sea urchins and sea stars. But from this variety, each individual usually specializes in only two to four kinds of prey. Sea otters frequently hunt in the kelp forests, usually in water less than 60 feet (18 meters) deep.

While sea otters hunt for food under water, they eat at the surface. An otter gathers its meal with its powerful forepaws or uses a rock to knock loose stubborn abalone and sea urchins. Back at the surface, the otter floats on its back and eats. It uses its powerful jaw muscles and blunt molars to crush its food. The otter may place a rock or other hard object on its chest to use as an anvil. Then the otter bashes its prey against the rock, breaking open hard-shelled animals like abalone, crabs and clams. Sea otters are the only marine mammals that use tools.

Reproduction

Sea otters mate year-round. A male and female bond together as a pair for a few days during mating activities.

After mating with one female, the male goes on to bond and mate with other females.

A female otter is pregnant for about six months and usually gives birth to a single pup a little bigger than a kitten, weighing about four or five pounds (two kilograms).

Female sea otters are generally excellent mothers. Males don't take part in caring for pups. The mother nurses the young pup for four to eight months on milk that contains 20 to 25 percent fat. (Cow's milk contains only three to four percent fat.) After one or two months, the pup begins eating solid food that its mother collects. By about three months of age, the pup can dive and begins learning how to hunt. A pup can usually hunt on its own by the time it's six months old.

Sea otters and people

Living so close to the coast makes sea otters very vulnerable to humans. Coastal Indians and northern Aleuts hunted sea otters for many thousands of years. At that time there were probably 18,000 to 20,000 otters living off the California coast and hundreds of thousands throughout their Pacific range.

In 1741 Russian hunters found the otters, and the commercial otter fur trade began. There was a great demand for the otters' beautiful, warm pelts in Russia, Europe, Japan and especially China. In the late 1700s, the Americans and English joined the hunt. By the early 1900s, sea otters were nearly extinct. In 1911, the International Fur Seal Treaty brought protection to the sea otter and other marine mammals.

Otters were thought to be extinct off the California coast until a group of about 50 otters along the Big Sur coast became publicly known in 1938. All the sea otters currently living along the central California coast descended from these few survivors. Since the late 1930s this population has been growing in number and expanding north and south along the coast.

By 1992, the sea otter population off the California coast had grown to about 2,100. However, they're still threatened by oil spills, gill nets and other human disturbances.

Explore Your Yard

MATERIALS
- Plastic milk jug
- Magnifying lens
- Magazines
- Scissors
- Crayons, colored pencils or colored markers
- Large sheets of plain paper

Take a walk through your backyard or school yard and look for insects, birds and other animals. If you'd like to look at them more closely, bring along a tray and magnifying lens to hold the plants and animals that you find.

To make a tray for observing the plants and animals you find, cut off the bottom of a plastic milk jug. Recycle the top half and use the bottom piece as a tray to hold plants and animals. When you're done observing, be sure to return any animals you collect back to their homes.

Compare how one kind of animal is different from and similar to another kind of animal. What makes a bird a bird? An insect an insect? A mammal a mammal? What kind of animal is a person? (A person is a mammal.) How are marine mammals different from land mammals? Back inside, use pictures from magazines and ones that you draw to make several collages with each collage illustrating a different kind of animal.

There's a Whale in Your Room!

MATERIALS

- Your favorite drawing or painting materials
- Construction paper in different colors
- Large sheet of butcher paper
- Marine Mammal Field Guide (pages 140–144)

Create a mural of mammals that live in the sea. Draw or paint a life-sized harbor seal, sea lion, sea otter, dolphin or other favorite marine mammal. If whales and orcas are too big to fit on your mural, just include the head or tail flukes coming onto or going off of the mural's edges. Use construction paper to cut out food that each animal eats (sea otters eat sea urchins and crabs) and to create each animal's habitat (sea otters live in kelp forests). Take a friend on a walk through your oceany room.

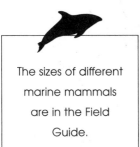

The sizes of different marine mammals are in the Field Guide.

What's for Dinner?

MATERIALS

- Scale to weigh yourself
- Paper
- Pencil
- A variety of utensils from your own and other cultures

Use a scale to compare your weight with that of a 60-pound (27 kilograms) sea otter and a 160-ton (45 metric tons) blue whale. Otters eat a quarter of their body weight each day; this otter would eat about 15 pounds (7 kilograms). Add up the weight of your lunch or dinner to see how many lunches or dinners this otter would eat in a day.

A blue whale eats four tons of krill a day to get three million calories. Calculate how many burgers, pizzas or milk shakes would satisfy that huge appetite.

Now collect a variety of utensils that you use to prepare and eat your food. What kinds of utensils do people from different cultures use? Compare the ways we eat food with the way an otter catches and eats its food. How does a blue whale eat? What kinds of body parts and behaviors help these animals eat?

Blue whale feeds on krill.

Take an Imaginary Trip

MATERIALS

- 4-5 sheets of white paper to make a log book
- Decorative paper for cover
- Heavy-duty needle and thread
- 12 inches of yarn
- Pencil and drawing materials
- Map of the west coast of North America, from Alaska to Baja California

TO MAKE YOUR LOG,

fold the sheets of white paper in half. Unfold them and cut along the crease. Stack the papers together and fold the decorative paper around them. Stitch the pages and cover together along the center fold.

Imagine you're on a boat following a young gray whale migrating from Alaska to Baja California. The journey takes about 12 weeks during the late fall and early winter. Keep a log of the whale's activities with words and pictures, recording one entry for each week of the long journey. Remember to write about the fishes and people the whale encounters and the adventures that take place during the trip. Find or draw a map that shows Alaska and Baja California to chart the course of your journey.

LOG BOOK

Who Lives Here?

MATERIALS
• Map of the area you're interested in studying
• Marine Mammal Field Guide (on pages 140–144) or pictures from magazines
• Paper
• Marking pens
• Glue

On a map, glue pictures of marine mammals to show where they live. Make a chart to show which ones live in the same area year-round and which ones migrate. (Pacific white-sided dolphins, porpoises, seals and sea otters live in Monterey Bay; sea lions, large whales and common dolphins visit during their migrations.)

Common dolphin

Monterey Bay Marine Mammals

Animal	YEAR-ROUND RESIDENT	VISITOR
Sea Otter	X	
Seal	X	
Porpoise	X	
Gray Whale		X
Common Dolphin		X

An Oily Mess

MATERIALS
- Vegetable oil
- Old bowl
- Variety of materials to drop in oil (feathers, fake fur, fabric)
- Variety of materials to clean up oil (soap, cotton balls)

Oil spills can be quite harmful to marine mammals. Sea otters, in particular, are in danger because they need clean fur to stay warm. Their thick, well-groomed fur makes a layer that keeps the cold ocean water from getting close to their skin. But if an otter's fur gets oily, it bunches up into clumps, exposing its skin to the cold water. With no way to stay warm, the otter may get sick and die. Pour some vegetable oil into an old bowl. Dip different kinds of materials, like feathers and fake fur, into the oil to see what happens. How would you clean the oil from these materials? How can people minimize the occurrence of oil spills?

Brown pelicans

There Aren't Many Left!

MATERIALS
- Magazines
- Scissors

Collect pictures of threatened animals, like the sea otter and grizzly bear. Are there threatened plants, too? Discuss why these plants and animals are threatened and how they're important to the environment. Plan a way you'd like to help threatened plants or animals. (You may wish to tell a friend, keep the plant or animal's home clean, buy products that don't harm the plant or animals or write letters to key decision makers.)

Do you think people should build houses on farm land where endangered or threatened animals live? If not, then where will people live and how will they make a living? If they build somewhere else, what about the animals that live there? What can we do?

Get Involved!

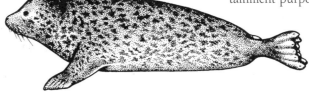

MATERIALS
- Paper
- Pencil

Write letters to organizations listed on Join A Group Working to Protect the Sea (page 221) to find out how you can help protect whales and other marine mammals. Use this information to make posters for your school or community, paint T-shirts and do other projects that share with people what you've learned about marine mammals, their loss of habitat and why they need protection.

What Do You Think?

MATERIALS
- Books or other information about federal laws that protect marine mammals

At the library, learn about the different federal laws that protect marine mammals. Do you think protected otter populations should be established on uninhabited islands if this practice threatens the local abalone fishing industry? Is traditional subsistence whaling by native groups justified? Should marine mammals be kept in captivity for educational and entertainment purposes?

Harbor seal

Minke whale

Ollie Otter Lunch Bag Puppet

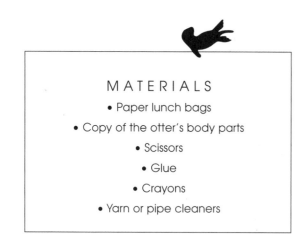

MATERIALS
- Paper lunch bags
- Copy of the otter's body parts
- Scissors
- Glue
- Crayons
- Yarn or pipe cleaners

To make Ollie Otter

Cut out the otter's body parts. Glue the otter's head to the bottom of the lunch bag. Use yarn or pipe cleaners to make whiskers. Then glue the tail to the inside edge of the bag and the rest of the parts to the outside. Color your otter with crayons: sea otters are brown-colored with a black nose; clams are yellow or tan. Have children use their puppets to act out the story below while you read it to them.

A sea otter's meal

A sea otter dives to the seafloor, searching for something to eat. Steering with its tail, the otter uses its rear flippers, which are webbed like a duck's feet, to paddle itself along. It spots a clam hidden just under the sand and quickly swims over to it. Wriggling its whiskers, the otter feels for the clam, then grabs it with its padded paws. The otter also picks up a small rock, then tucks the rock and the clam in a fold of skin under its arm.

The otter swims back to the surface and floats on its back. Setting the rock on its chest as if it's a table, the otter holds the clam and bangs it against the rock to crack open the clam's hard shell. The otter tears at the soft clam body inside the shell with its sharp teeth in front, then chews the clam with its strong jaws and flat teeth that are in back.

Feeling full, the otter rubs its face and chest with its paws, cleaning its fur from any leftovers. Then the otter rests, floating on its back in the warm sun.

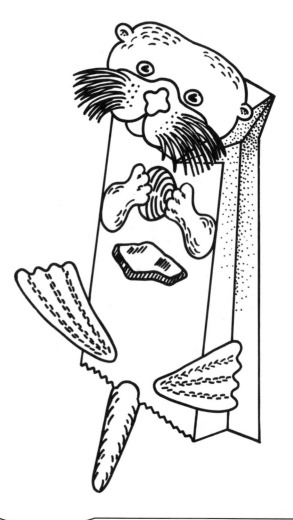

Puppet pieces

tail

whiskers

paw

flipper

clam

paw

rock

flipper

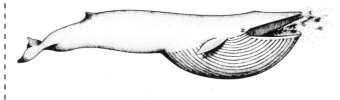

Blue whale

Balaenoptera musculus SIZE: TO 100 FT. (30.5 M)
Largest of all living animals, the 160-ton blue whale consumes some of the smallest prey. Lunging open-mouthed at schools of shrimplike krill, this baleen whale can engulf and strain four tons of food daily.
The 24-foot-long newborn blue whale is an impressive eater, too. Drinking 130 gallons of milk a day, the calf can double its weight in one week.

California sea lion

Zalophus californianus SIZE: TO 7.5 FT. (2.3 M)
Diving 800 feet deep, the sea lion paddles with its strong, front limbs and steers with its rear flippers. On land, it rotates the hind flippers forward to walk on all fours. At mating time, the male sea lion barks and bellows to establish his territory and gather a harem of females. Never giving ground, not even to eat, the bull defends his turf from male intruders.

Common dolphin

Delphinus delphis SIZE: TO 8.5 FT. (2.6 M)
These slender dolphins live and travel in huge groups. Even in pods of a hundred or more, the dolphins protect each other. When one is injured, the others take turns supporting it so it doesn't drown. In some countries, people still hunt and eat dolphins. Thousands more—accidentally caught in fish nets—die each year.

Dall's porpoise

Phocoenoides dalli SIZE: TO 7 FT. (2.1 M)

This stocky porpoise has a small dorsal fin and tiny flippers, but it's a spectacular swimmer. Moving like a hydroplane, it races through the water, leaving behind a "rooster tail" of spray when it surfaces for air. For food, the Dall's porpoise favors deep sea fishing. It roams out beyond the continental shelf to hunt for squids, crustaceans and fishes.

Fin whale

Balaenoptera physalus SIZE: TO 88 FT. (27 M)

The world's second largest animal, the fin whale can cruise the open sea at speeds of 35 miles an hour. Most other whales can't swim this fast for extended periods. Uneven coloring makes the fin whale unique among all whales; its lower jaw is white on the right and black on the left. Dark and light patterns on its body may disguise the fin whale as it hunts fishes.

Gray whale

Eschrichtius robustus SIZE: TO 50 FT. (15 M)

Gray whales make the longest migration of any mammal, swimming more than 10,000 miles each year. In fall, they head south to their breeding areas off Baja California; in spring, they return north to feed in the Bering Sea. Unlike other baleen whales, the gray whale eats bottom-living crustaceans. The whale sucks in a mouthful of mud and strains it through the baleen to remove the prey.

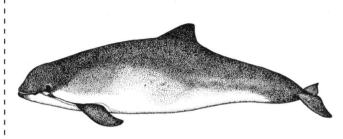

Harbor porpoise

Phocoena phocoena SIZE: TO 6 FT. (1.8 M)
The stocky harbor porpoise lives near shore in harbors, bays and river mouths. Wary of boats, it won't cruise alongside them, preferring to swim quietly on the surface. Harbor porpoises work cooperatively to hunt squids and fishes. The porpoises herd a school of fish into a tight ball, then each porpoise grabs a fish headfirst and swallows it whole.

Harbor seal

Phoca vitulina SIZE: TO 5 FT. (1.5 M)
A harbor seal can't "walk" on land the way a sea lion can. On shore, the harbor seal has to inch along awkwardly on its belly. But in water, it's a graceful swimmer, powered by its webbed, hind flippers. Harbor seals don't migrate far from home. They hunt fishes, squids and octopuses near shore, using their large eyes and sensitive whiskers to help them locate prey.

Humpback whale

Megaptera novaeangliae SIZE: TO 51 FT. (15.6 M)
Humpback whales travel between their Arctic feeding grounds and tropical breeding grounds. Some migrate to Hawaii and some to Mexico; a few visit both sites in different years. In the breeding areas, the males display their great vocal range with songs that may warn off other males or attract females. As they sing, the whales gradually alter their song, so each year it's a different melody.

Minke whale

Balaenoptera acutorostrata SIZE: TO 35 FT. (10.7 M)
Although it's as long as a bus, the minke whale is the smallest of the baleen whales. As agile as a porpoise, it can leap from the water in a graceful arc or ride the bow wave of a passing ship. Alone or with a companion, the minke whale hunts squids, fishes and krill. The whale jumps and splashes to gather its prey in a ball, then lunges in to scoop up the cluster of food.

Northern elephant seal

Mirounga angustirostris SIZE: TO 19.5 FT. (5.9 M)
Once hunted to near-extinction, elephant seals are now breeding successfully again. At mating time, they move ashore, the males battling for position. With snorts of warning, the dominant bulls defend their females against rival males. After breeding, the elephant seals return to the sea to feed. Diving deeper than 2,700 feet, they hunt deepwater fishes and squids.

Pacific white-sided dolphin

Lagenorhynchus obliquidens SIZE: TO 7 FT. (2.1 M)
Resident pods of hundreds of white-sided dolphins streak through the water. They swim in formation with other dolphins and sea lions, sometimes leaping from the water in spirited somersaults. Each dolphin is unique, from the patterns on its body to the noises it makes. High-pitched squeaks, clicks and whistles help it communicate with its family pod.

Sea otter

Enhydra lutris SIZE: TO 5.5 FT. (1.7 M)

For warmth, the sea otter relies on its thick, fur coat which has between 170,000 and one million hairs per square inch. The otter spends nearly half its waking hours grooming its fur coat to keep it waterproof. The otter dives for shellfish, then eats lying on its back at the surface. Because it consumes abalones and crabs, the otter sometimes competes with people for food.

Sei whale

Balaenoptera borealis SIZE: TO 60 FT. (18.5 M)

Sei whales cruise the oceans from polar regions to the tropics. Unlike other baleen whales, they don't have predictable migration routes but seem to follow their prey, trailing the northward fish migrations. Swimming near the surface, the whale skims small invertebrates from the sea. As it feeds, the whale's throat pleats expand like an accordion to hold tons of water and prey.

Sperm whale

Physeter macrocephalus SIZE: TO 62 FT. (18.9 M)

Diving a mile or more below the surface, the sperm whale makes clicking noises to echolocate for prey. When it finds a shark or giant squid, the whale stuns it with a blast of sound and swallows it whole. For years, whalers hunted this whale for the milk-colored oil that fills its huge, square head. No one knows what the oil is for; perhaps it helps the whale focus sounds.

SEARCHING FOR SEA LIFE

Fishes

What Is a Fish?

Beneath the water's surface lives an animal that's adapted to a purely aquatic life: the fish. Like other animals, a fish breathes, feeds, moves, reproduces and senses its surroundings, but it is designed to do all these in water.

Next time you're in a swimming pool or at the beach, try walking through the water. Because water is 800 times denser than air, your legs have to push the water aside, making it hard for you— or any animal—to move through it. But a fish's torpedo-shaped body is adapted to slice through water with minimal resistance.

Fishes propel and balance themselves with fins and take dissolved oxygen out of the water using gills. A backbone provides a place of attachment for swimming muscles. Most fishes have scales for protection, and some have a balloonlike swimbladder that helps them stay at any depth without sinking or rising.

The first vertebrates, fishes evolved from marine invertebrates (animals without backbones) about 500 million years ago. Ichthyologists (people who study fishes) have identified more than 20,000 species; that's more than all the other species of vertebrates put together. New species are discovered every year, and there are many more we don't even know about.

Three main groups of fishes are living today: jawless fishes, like lampreys and hagfishes; cartilaginous fishes, like sharks, skates and rays; and bony fishes, like rockfishes, tunas and eels. Most fishes are bony fishes, the same kind that comes to many people's minds when asked to picture a typical fish.

Adaptations to aquatic life

Take a look at two or three different fishes and you'll see how each is specially adapted to its surroundings. Each species is the result of evolution over millions of years and has its own body shape, color, body parts (like fins and mouth) and even behaviors. The designs we see today reflect each fish's habitat: the substrate, properties of water and availability of food.

Body shape

The basic torpedo-shaped body varies according to where in the ocean the fish lives and how it makes its living. The sleek bodies of fast-swimming fishes like tunas and mackerel can zip through the open sea at 50 miles per hour with little resistance. Less streamlined fishes depend on other ways to catch food and avoid being eaten.

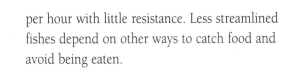

California sheephead

The scorpion fish, with its poisonous spines and camouflaged coloration, lies motionless among rocks to escape detection.

Some fishes, like the flounder, halibut and sanddab, are adapted to live on the seafloor. These flatfishes start life with bodies shaped like a typical fish. But as the young flatfish grows, one eye migrates to the other side of its head and its body flattens side-to-side. The adult flatfish lies on one side of its body with both eyes on the other side to see what's going on above.

Swimbladder

Many bony fishes have a balloonlike swimbladder that makes them weightless in water. By regulating the amount of gas in this air-tight sac, a fish can stay at any depth without sinking or rising. Most bottom-dwellers don't have swimbladders because they stay on the bottom.

Gills

Unlike marine mammals that surface for air, fishes breathe under water. A fish absorbs the water's dissolved oxygen by passing water through its mouth and across tiny gill membranes containing blood vessels. The blood releases carbon dioxide and takes up oxygen that's carried throughout the fish's body.

Scales

Tough, flexible scales overlap one another, serving as a coat of armor to protect most fishes. A layer of slime covers the scales, helping the fish move more smoothly through the water and protecting it from infection. Some fishes, like the wolf-eel that hides in caves, have no scales at all and protect themselves in other ways.

Fins

A fish's fins are specialized according to where and how the fish lives. Operated by muscles, all fins have a particular job. Some fishes have modified fins, an adaptation that helps the fish survive. The anglerfish lures its prey with a modified dorsal fin: it dangles the fin like a fishing line with bait in front of its large mouth.

Lateral line

A fish's lateral line detects the slightest water movements. Special sense organs lie in tiny pits along the fish's side, forming a visible line. These organs give fishes a sense of distant touch that may help them detect approaching predators or prey and stay close together when schooling.

Mouth

The size, shape and position of a fish's mouth depend on the size of food eaten and where it finds its food. Most fishes, like a rockfish, salmon and surfperch, have mouths in front of their heads to pick at or chase food that's in front of them. Others, like the hatchetfish, have upward-pointing mouths to catch prey swimming above. In the deep sea where food is scarce, a fish like the gulper eel, with its huge mouth and unhinging jaw, can swallow a fish larger than itself.

Dorsal and anal fins

The dorsal and anal fins on most fishes work together like a boat's keel, keeping the fish from rolling over. On other fishes, like the pipefish and ocean sunfish, these fins propel.

Pectoral fin

Some fishes use their pair of pectoral fins to stabilize and steer, while others, like the sheephead, propel themselves with these fins.

Caudal fin

The square caudal fin of this rockfish helps it move with short, quick bursts, while the forked caudal fin of a mackerel propels it faster over greater distances.

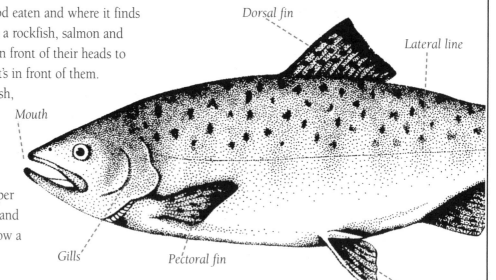

Dorsal fin

Lateral line

Mouth

Gills

Pectoral fin

Pelvic fin

Protection

Fishes have a variety of adaptations that protect them from predators. Many are camouflaged: their body shapes, patterns and colors help them blend in with their surroundings. A wolf-eel's ribbonlike body shape helps it hide in crevices. A flatfish, living on the seafloor, can change its patterns to match the seafloor's variety of colors. Open sea fishes, like tunas and sardines, have countershaded coloring: dark-colored on top to help them hide from predators looking down, but light on the underside to blend in with light streaming from above. Other fishes can be venomous, like the scorpionfish with its poisonous spines.

Behavioral adaptations also protect fishes. Some fishes school: a mackerel swimming in schools with several thousand individuals may be harder for a predator to catch than when it's alone. The mass of darting fishes may confuse the predator.

Reproduction

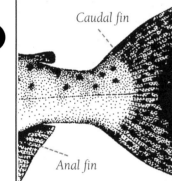

Caudal fin

Anal fin

King salmon

Fishes must successfully reproduce to help keep their populations healthy. Most fishes, like the flounder and mackerel, broadcast thousands of eggs and sperm to drift in the ocean's currents. Some, like most sharks and rays, bear a few live young. Others, like the lingcod, guard a nest of eggs on the seafloor until they hatch. Still others, like the pipefish, reverse the male and female roles: the males raise their young in a pouch. The sheephead has an unusual adaptation: all are born as females. When they reach a foot in length, they can change their sex to male if no other males are around.

People and fishes

For thousands of years, people have fished the ocean's waters, mainly for food. In Monterey Bay, California, a booming sardine industry lasted nearly half a century, providing food and a living for many people. But a combination of factors, including overfishing, caused the industry to collapse in the 1940s.

Throughout time, many waters worldwide have been overfished. Today, we continue to struggle with finding and maintaining a balance between how many fishes can be taken and how many need to remain in the sea to keep the populations healthy. Some countries have laws that govern the size and number of fishes that can be taken and where they can be fished. Other laws regulate the amount and kinds of waste that can be released into the ocean, rivers and lakes.

Scientists continue to study fishes, learning how they interact with each other and with their environment. Such research helps determine how many fishes can be taken without damaging their populations. High levels of pollutants and an ever-growing world population still threaten the world's fishes. With continued protection and research, perhaps fish populations can remain healthy while providing food and resources for people. The future of the sea's fishes depends on management and lifestyle decisions people make today.

A Fish Is a Fish

MATERIALS
• Paper and pencil or chalkboard and chalk

Draw a blank fish body on a piece of paper or chalkboard and label the body parts. What body parts does a fish use to swim? What does it need to breathe? How does it protect itself? How does it sense its surroundings? What body parts does it use to catch and eat its food? Design and draw an imaginary fish, then explain the way it swims, catches its food and hides from predators.

A Scientist's Clues

MATERIALS
• Yourself and a friend
• Pictures of several different kinds of fishes

Why do scientists describe animals in detail to help them with their studies? To begin, pretend you're a scientist. Choose an object and describe its color, shape, size and your feelings about it to a friend. Have your friend try to guess the object. Switch roles to let your friend describe an object while you guess. Do this several times until you both feel comfortable knowing the kinds of details and the level of detail that's needed to accurately describe an object to someone else. Now, compare pictures of two different fishes. Describe several ways the fishes are similar. How are they different?

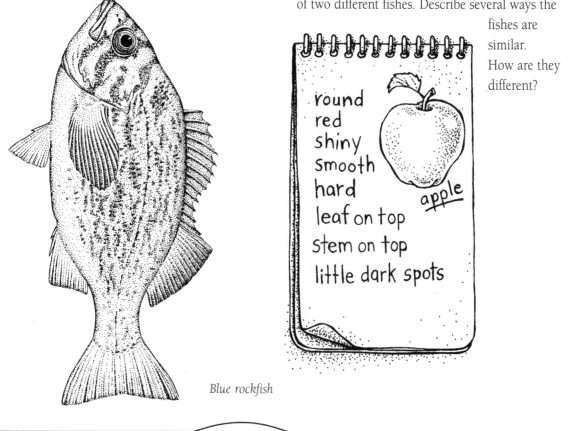

round
red
shiny
smooth
hard
leaf on top
stem on top
little dark spots

apple

Blue rockfish

Raising Fish

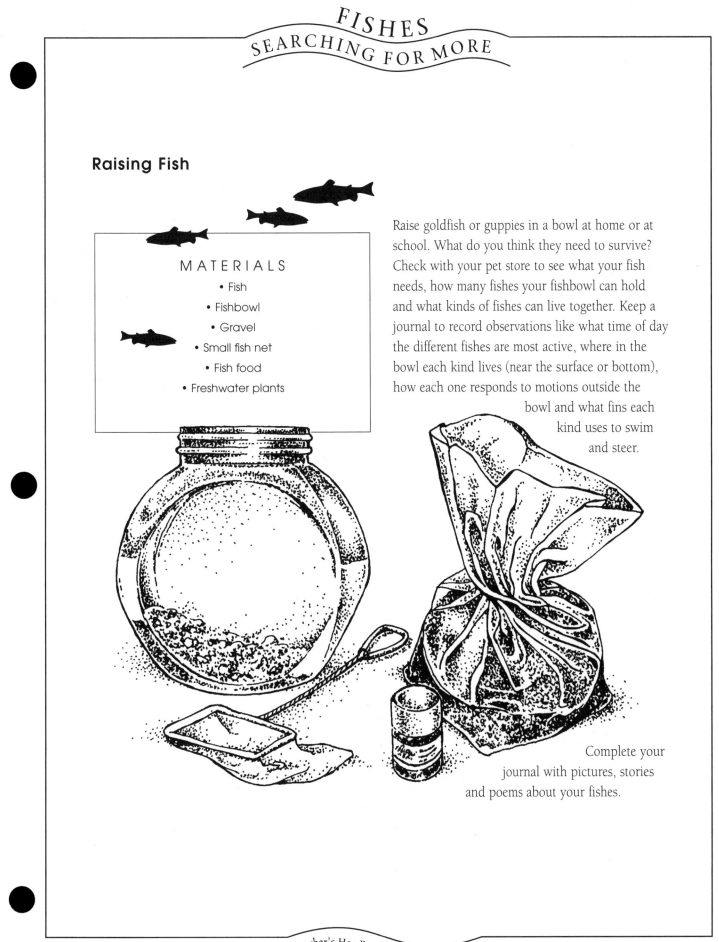

MATERIALS
- Fish
- Fishbowl
- Gravel
- Small fish net
- Fish food
- Freshwater plants

Raise goldfish or guppies in a bowl at home or at school. What do you think they need to survive? Check with your pet store to see what your fish needs, how many fishes your fishbowl can hold and what kinds of fishes can live together. Keep a journal to record observations like what time of day the different fishes are most active, where in the bowl each kind lives (near the surface or bottom), how each one responds to motions outside the bowl and what fins each kind uses to swim and steer.

Complete your journal with pictures, stories and poems about your fishes.

Design an Aquarium

Here's your chance to design your own aquarium exhibit! Make a diorama (in a shoe box) or draw a picture of an ocean habitat. Create plants and animals for the habitat, and write labels to describe your exhibit. As you write your labels, think about how much time a person might spend reading each one. What are the most important things you'd like other people to learn about the sea? What are the best ways to say these things? How can you say them in as few words as possible?

MATERIALS

- Shoe box or other cardboard box
- Construction paper
- Favorite arts and crafts materials
- Scissors
- Glue

FISH FINGER PUPPETS

Use pieces of felt and fabric to create fish finger puppets (and other sea life!). Put on a puppet show in front of your exhibit, teaching your friends and family about fishes and the ocean.

In this diorama, a thresher shark swims through the sea, while a brown pelican flies above.

To Market, To Market

MATERIALS
• Yourself

Visit a fish market and choose something you'd like to eat. Find the fish's name, where it was caught and what kind of fishing method was used to catch it. Talk to at least two restaurant fish buyers, fish market keepers, other fish buyers or fishermen and ask them how the numbers and kinds of seafood have changed over the last year. How have numbers and kinds of seafood changed year-to-year during their careers? What do you think is causing these changes? Are those things still occurring and causing more change? Are the changes for the benefit of the ocean and the planet or not? What are some ways people could influence these changes?

What Do You Think?

How would you feel if your favorite kind of fish were threatened by overfishing or pollution? How could you help save it? How is the fish important to the sea? How is it important to people? How can the species be safe in its sea home and fished at the same time?

Blue rockfish

King salmon

California halibut

Fish Bingo

Take this with you on your next visit to an aquarium!

The sea is home to hundreds of different kinds of fishes, each with its own shape, size and color. To explore this wonderful world of animals, look for the fishes that these clues describe. When you find a fish, draw its picture or write its name in the box with its clue. Three in a row makes Bingo! Can you find all the fishes?

A fish chasing another fish.	A fish that blends in with where it lives.	A fish with coloration that helps it hide in the open sea. (Hint: dark on top, light on its belly.)
A fish hiding in kelp or other seaweed.	A school of fishes.	A fish that rests on its fins.
A flat fish living on the sandy seafloor.	A snakelike fish that can escape into rock crevices.	A fish with a body shaped for fast swimming.

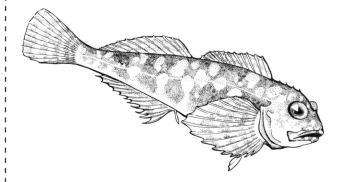

Tidepool sculpin

Oligocottus maculosus SIZE: TO 3.5 IN. (9 CM)
A tidepool sculpin is hard to see because it's the same color as the rocks and plants around it. This fish can be grassy green, spotted brown or bright red. Why do you think it's hiding?

Blue rockfish

Sebastes mystinus SIZE: TO 21 IN. (53 CM)
Blue rockfish swim among the kelp plants. They hunt small floating animals there. Rockfishes have poisonous spines on their fins for protection.

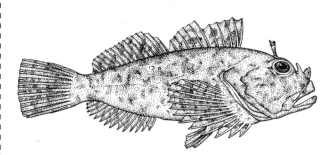

Cabezon

Scorpaenichthys marmoratus
SIZE: TO 3.25 FT. (99 CM)
Cabezon means big head in Spanish. This fish has a big mouth, too—it can gulp large prey. Cabezons often swallow whole abalones. Then they spit out the shells.

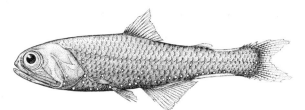

Lanternfish

Stenobrachius leucopsarus SIZE: TO 5 IN. (13 CM)
The flash of a lanternfish is a message in code to
other fishes. Each kind of lanternfish flashes its own
pattern of lights to attract the right mate. Some
lanternfish can light up their tongues to attract prey.

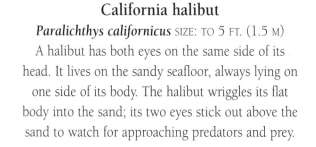

California halibut

Paralichthys californicus SIZE: TO 5 FT. (1.5 M)
A halibut has both eyes on the same side of its
head. It lives on the sandy seafloor, always lying on
one side of its body. The halibut wriggles its flat
body into the sand; its two eyes stick out above the
sand to watch for approaching predators and prey.

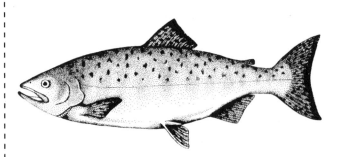

King salmon

Oncorhynchus tshawytscha SIZE: TO 5 FT. (1.5 M)
Salmon are born in freshwater rivers, then swim to
the salty sea where they spend most of their lives.
As adults, they must return to the river to lay eggs.
Salmon can find the way to their home streams
from thousands of miles out in the ocean.

SEARCHING

FOR

SEA LIFE

Sharks, Skates and Rays

Spiny dogfish

What Is a Shark?

For 350 million years, sharks and their kin have been swimming the seas. Sharks have always inspired our admiration and fear, but for all our fascination with them, we still know surprisingly little about their lives.

Sharks swim in all the world's oceans—even some freshwater rivers and lakes. There are about 800 species of sharks, skates and rays worldwide and about 25 species in Monterey Bay, California.

Unlike most fishes, whose skeletons are made of bone, sharks and their kin have skeletons of cartilage. (Their class, Chondrichthyes, means cartilaginous fishes.) Other features that set them apart from bony fishes are their reproductive techniques (all use internal fertilization), skin covered with toothlike dermal denticles (not scales) and five to seven pairs of gill slits (gills without covers).

Though sharks, skates and rays are closely related, many differences distinguish them from one another. Most sharks have streamlined, torpedo-shaped bodies, while skates and rays are flattened and have disc- or diamond-shaped bodies. Rays have blunt noses and smooth skin; skates have pointed noses and rough or spiny skin. Another major difference is that skates lay eggs and rays give birth to live young. Sharks may do either, depending on the species.

Adaptations for survival

Sharks are remarkably well-adapted for their varied lifestyles. Cartilaginous skeletons and huge oily livers help increase the buoyancy of open sea swimmers like the blue shark. An adaptation that helps sharks, skates and rays succeed as predators is the ability to replace worn and missing teeth. Numerous rows of new, growing teeth line up behind the front teeth; as a tooth is worn or lost, the one behind it moves forward to take its place.

Big skate

Big skates egg case

Sharks, skates and rays have a wider range of sensory abilities than any other group of fishes. They sense their surroundings and find prey through taste and smell, their chemical-sensitive skin and tiny cup-shaped pores, called pit organs, scattered over the skin's surface.

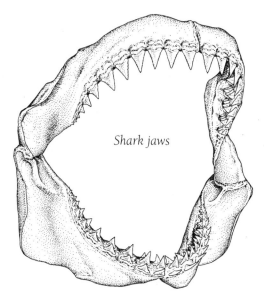

Shark jaws

Under a microscope, these pores look like tiny taste buds, but researchers don't fully understand their function. Some think these pores may indeed be taste buds; others think they detect vibrations. A shark can detect predators and prey at close range by sensing the electrical impulses and tiny changes in water motion made by other animals. Most sharks, skates and rays also have good vision and excellent hearing.

Clues to lifestyles

Look at the teeth and body shape of a shark, skate or ray and you can guess where it lives, how it moves and what it eats. The streamlined shape of open sea sharks, like the white shark, is a clue that they can swim quickly and smoothly through the water to capture fast-moving prey. The razor-sharp teeth indicate their prey is large enough to be grasped and cut before swallowing.

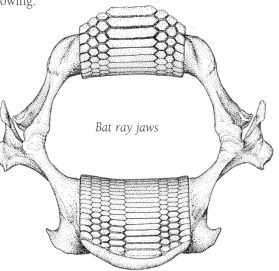

Bat ray jaws

From the flat body, slow swimming style and pavementlike teeth of a bat ray, you can deduce it spends a lot of time on the seafloor.

There the ray grinds up bottom-dwelling clams, crabs and worms, instead of chasing faster fishes.

Bat ray

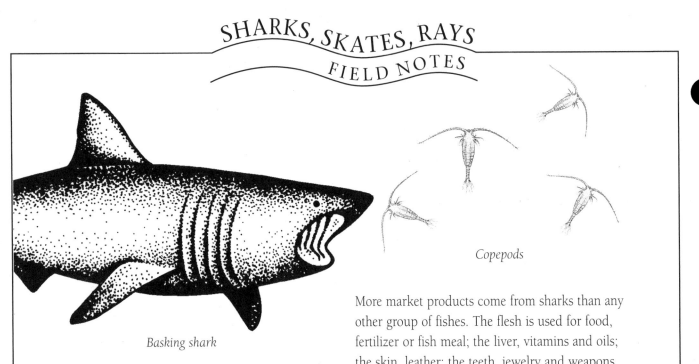

Basking shark

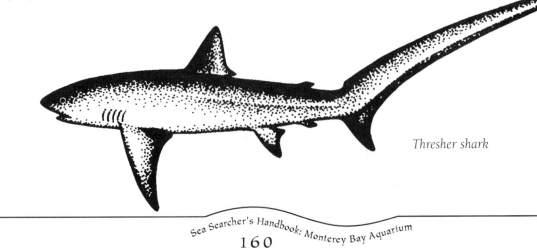

Copepods

A shark's size indicates its diet, but not always in the way you might think. The largest sharks eat the smallest prey. The 45-foot-long basking shark, the largest in Monterey Bay, has filtering gill rakers and hundreds of tiny teeth suited not for catching large prey, but for sieving tiny fishes and invertebrates.

Sharks and people

Though many people think of sharks as vicious killers, fewer than 30 people per year worldwide are attacked by sharks. Only 68 of the 350 known species are dangerous or potentially dangerous to humans. Statistics on sharks caught by fishermen show sharks have more to fear from people than people have to fear from sharks. To even the score, sharks would have to "catch" 4.5 million people per year.

More market products come from sharks than any other group of fishes. The flesh is used for food, fertilizer or fish meal; the liver, vitamins and oils; the skin, leather; the teeth, jewelry and weapons. And besides being a popular sport fish, they're used for medical research and biology and anatomy courses. Harpoon fishermen once hunted basking sharks in the bay, obtaining 200-400 gallons of liver oil from each. Spiny dogfish and soupfin sharks were also fished extensively off the central California coast for oil and meat. Today leopard, thresher, soupfin, bonito and blue sharks as well as skates are caught in the bay and sold in local fish markets.

Because sharks, skates and rays bear few young (which grow and mature slowly) overfishing can greatly reduce their numbers. By studying how these fishes grow, age and reproduce, scientists and regulating agencies hope to manage them in a way that keeps both shark fisheries and shark populations healthy.

Thresher shark

Who Likes Sharks?

MATERIALS
- Paper
- Pen or pencil
- Graph paper

Conduct a survey of your own and other people's attitudes towards sharks. Record responses of "strongly agree," "agree," "disagree" and "strongly disagree" to statements like: "I'm afraid of sharks," "Sharks are a major menace to humans," or "Most sharks are very large." Make a bar graph that shows the frequency of each of the four responses to your questions. What's the general attitude toward sharks? How do you feel about this? How do people use sharks and shark products? (People use sharks for sportfishing and research; and they use sharks for commercial products like shark liver oil, shark cartilage, oil and meat.)

START A SHARK CAMPAIGN!

What do you think would be the best way to educate people about sharks? Consider doing things like making "Save the Shark" posters to hang on school walls, writing radio spots and TV commercials, producing music and videos to share with your class, family or friends, decorating T-shirts and sending letters to elected officials, magazines and the editors of local newspapers.

Do you like sharks?

STATEMENT	RESPONSE			
	Strongly agree	Agree	Disagree	Strongly disagree
I'm afraid of sharks.		X		
All sharks attack people.				X
Sharks play an important role in nature.	X			
I like sharks.	X			
Most sharks are very large.			X	

Shark Math

MATERIALS
- Paper
- Pen or pencil
- Graph paper

Imagine you're a research biologist. Your studies show there are 10,000 bat rays in your local bay and the population is growing one percent per year. If a fishery for bat rays opens next year and removes three percent of the population each year, how long will it be before half the population is gone? Make a bar graph to show the total population each year for the next six years. (Begin this year with 10,000 bat rays.) Make another graph of the population if there were no fishery. What limits would you set on the number of bat rays which could be caught each year to protect the rays and the fishermen?

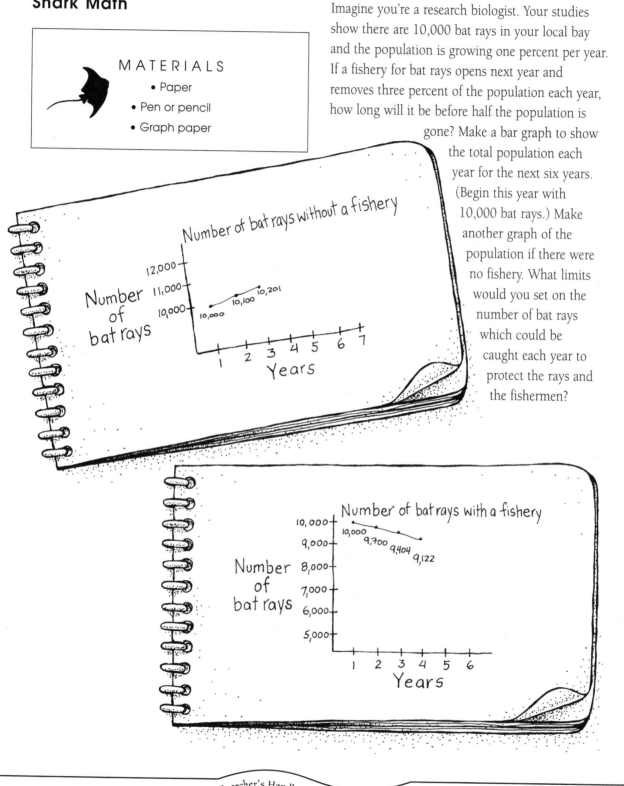

Number of bat rays without a fishery

Number of bat rays

12,000
11,000
10,000

10,000   10,100 10,201

1 2 3 4 5 6 7
Years

Number of bat rays with a fishery

Number of bat rays

10,000
9,000
8,000
7,000
6,000
5,000

10,000
9,700 9,404 9,122

1 2 3 4 5 6
Years

Sidewalk Sharks

MATERIALS

- Sidewalk chalk
- Sharks Field Guide (on pages 166–170)

The largest shark in Monterey Bay is the basking shark (45 feet) and the smallest is the filetail catshark (two feet). The largest shark in the world is the whale shark (60 feet).

On the sidewalk or on the blacktop at a playground or school yard, mark with chalk the length of these sharks. How tall are you? Compare these to the lengths of the other sharks in the Shark Field Guide. What's the largest shark in the waters nearest you?

Whale shark/60 feet

Basking shark/45 feet

Kid/3 feet

Filetail shark/2 feet

Design a Shark

Invent, draw or build an ocean habitat and a shark, skate or ray adapted for life there. Use a shoe box or other container to create the habitat and list the habitat's major characteristics. For instance, the deep sea is cold and has little or no light. How is your animal adapted to find and catch food? How does it protect itself, reproduce and cope with its habitat's conditions?

Shark Trivia

• What is a shark's skeleton made of?

• How does a shark detect its prey?

• What is the largest shark?

Design a shark trivia game. Use the information in the Shark Field Notes and Field Guide to write trivia questions, then hold a competition with your friends, family or classmates.

A Shark's Story

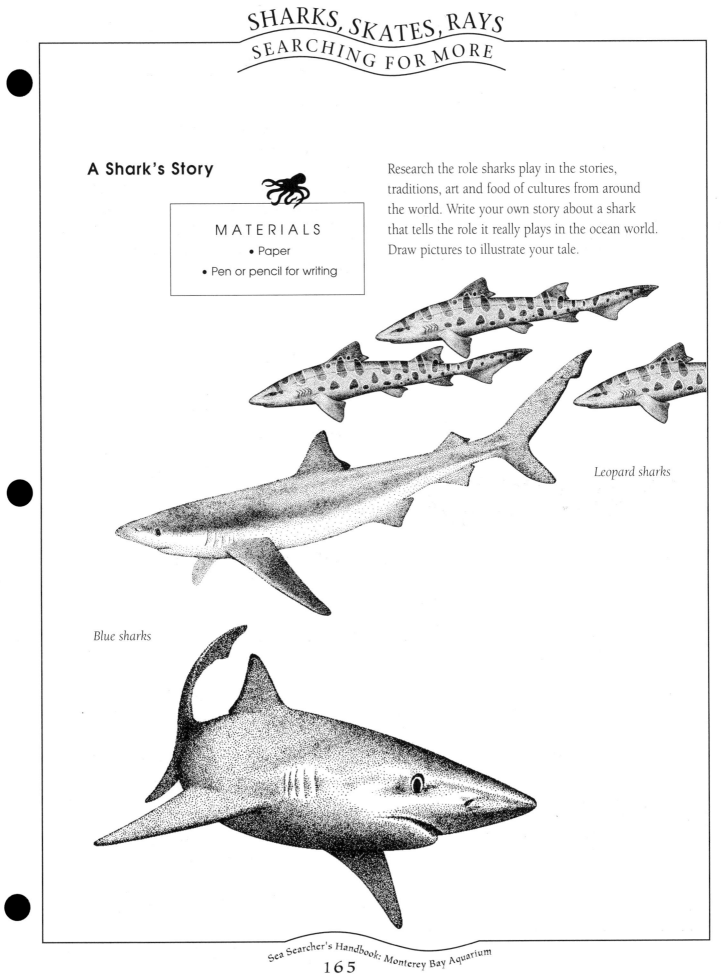

MATERIALS
- Paper
- Pen or pencil for writing

Research the role sharks play in the stories, traditions, art and food of cultures from around the world. Write your own story about a shark that tells the role it really plays in the ocean world. Draw pictures to illustrate your tale.

Leopard sharks

Blue sharks

Leopard shark

Triakis semifasciata SIZE: TO 7 FT. (2.1 M)
Leopard sharks live on sandy or rocky bottoms of bays or other inshore areas. Their spotted and barred coloring camouflages them against the seafloor. Leopard sharks eat fishes, fish eggs and invertebrates like crabs, worms and shrimps. Sevengills and other large sharks prey on leopard sharks.

Sevengill shark

Notorynchus cepedianus SIZE: TO 9 FT. (2.7 M)
Sevengill sharks often live in shallow bays. They have seven gills on each side of the body, unlike most sharks, which have five. Because of their bulky bodies, sevengills and their relatives are called "cow sharks." Sevengills eat crabs and fishes (including small sharks, skates and rays) as well as dead animals.

Blue shark

Prionace glauca SIZE: TO 13.5 FT. (4 M)
Blue sharks usually live offshore but visit the nearshore waters of Monterey Bay in late summer and fall. They make seasonal migrations of thousands of miles. Sleek and graceful, they use their front fins for gliding, a swimming method that is especially efficient at low speeds. Blue sharks feed mostly on fishes and squid.

Horn shark

Heterodontus francisci SIZE: TO 4 FT. (1.2 M)

Horn sharks live on the bottom near shore, in rocky or sandy areas or in kelp forests. Their spots serve as camouflage, while flexible lower fins help them move easily over the seafloor. Horn sharks eat small fishes and invertebrates such as shrimp and clams. Their low, flat back teeth help crush the shells of their prey.

Thresher shark

Alopias vulpinus SIZE: TO 20 FT. (6 M)

Thresher sharks live in the open sea, sometimes coming closer to shore as they hunt. Their young are often found inshore off beaches and in bays. They eat fishes, squid and other animals of the open sea. Biologists think thresher sharks use the long upper part of the tail to round up and stun prey. These sharks are caught by commercial fishermen for food.

White shark

Carcharodon carcharias SIZE: TO 30 FT. (9.1 M)

White sharks live both offshore and near the coast. They are fast, efficient swimmers. Their torpedo-shaped bodies and symmetrical tails are adaptations for speed. White sharks eat fishes (including sharks), seabirds and mammals, turtles and shellfish. They're responsible for most shark attacks on humans.

Spiny dogfish

Squalus acanthias SIZE: TO 5 FT. (1.5 M)

Spiny dogfish live in schools, both near the coast (often in bays) and offshore as deep as 2,400 feet (732 meters). They've been known to live 80 years or more. A spiny dogfish has one poisonous spine 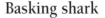 in front of each dorsal fin. They eat small fishes and invertebrates like crabs and shrimps; they're also caught by fishermen for food.

Basking shark

Cetorhinus maximus SIZE: TO 45 FT. (13.7 M)

These large sharks live both offshore and near the coast and are often seen near the surface. Basking sharks eat zooplankton (small, drifting animals like shrimp). To gather and strain their food, basking sharks have large mouths and long, stiff, hairlike projections called gill rakers lining their gills. Their numerous teeth are tiny.

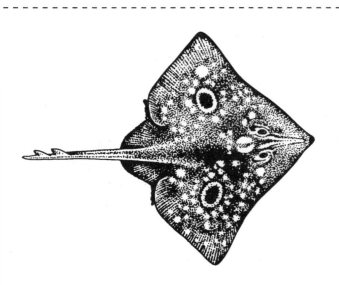

Big skate

Raja binoculata SIZE: TO 8 FT. (2.4 M) WIDE

The largest skate in the area, big skates live on the bottom in shallow water, to 360 feet (110 meters). Instead of giving birth to live young, they lay egg cases called "mermaid's purses." Big skates eat fishes, crabs and shrimp. Their predators include sevengill sharks. Fishermen also catch skates. The "wings" of the skate are the part that people like to eat most.

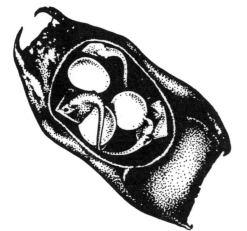

Skate egg case

Raja binoculata SIZE: TO 12 IN. (30 CM)

Instead of giving birth to live young, skates lay a tough egg case containing one to seven skate embryos. The egg case ("mermaid's purse") has hooked corners that may help it catch in seaweed on the sand. The young skates grow and develop for many months, each nourished by a yolk. This picture gives you a cutaway view of the case.

Thornback ray

Platyrhinoidis triseriata SIZE: TO 3 FT. (91 CM)

Thornback rays live on mud or sandy bottoms in shallow, nearshore areas to 150 feet (46 meters). They are often found off beaches or in bays, where they bury themselves in the sediment. These rays eat sand-dwelling invertebrates like shrimps, clams and worms. The rows of hooked spines on their backs are probably for defense.

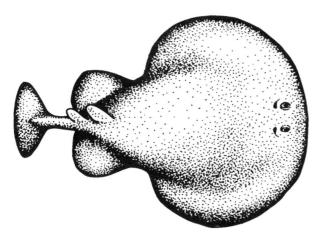

Pacific electric ray

Torpedo californica SIZE: TO 5 FT. (1.5 M)

Electric rays live on fine, sandy bottoms, often in kelp forests or near rocky reefs. They prefer shallow to moderately deep water, to 640 feet (195 meters). Electric rays eat mostly fishes. Though they're soft-bodied and slow-moving, these rays can stun prey and fend off enemies with electric shocks of up to 200 volts.

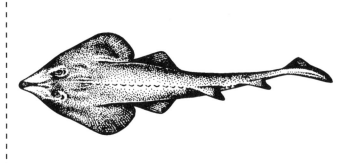

Shovelnose guitarfish

Rhinobatos productus SIZE: TO 6 FT. (1.8 M)
Shovelnose guitarfish live on muddy or sandy bottoms inshore and in bays, burrowing in the sand when they're resting. They prefer shallow water, to 50 feet (15 meters). Guitarfish eat small fishes and invertebrates like crabs, worms and shrimp. Their teeth are small and blunt for crushing their prey.

Bat ray

Myliobatis californica SIZE: TO 6 FT. (1.8 M) WIDE
Bat rays live on the bottom of sandy or muddy bays and sloughs, rocky areas and kelp forests. They're found in shallow water, to 150 feet (46 meters). A bat ray preys on invertebrates like clams, shrimp and worms. Flapping its wings to clear away mud, the ray sucks up its prey, crushing the shell with strong jaws and pavementlike teeth.

Filetail catshark

Parmaturus xaniurus SIZE: TO 22 IN. (56 CM)
A filetail catshark swims gracefully along the muddy seafloor. Gray-brown above and pale below, this fish blends in with its benthic habitat. Its large green eyes look upward, unlike those of shallow-water sharks. Catsharks lay eggs with curly corners. The curls catch on edges of rocks and sponges to anchor the egg case near the deep seafloor. Here it'll stay for two years while a tiny catshark grows inside.

"Be content with a little light,
So be it your own.
Explore, and explore"

RALPH WALDO EMERSON (1803-1882)
LITERARY ETHICS

SEARCHING FOR INTERACTIONS

SEARCHING FOR INTERACTIONS

Food Webs in the Sea

Food Webs in the Sea

Oceans are vast, complex worlds, teeming with life forms of all shapes, colors and sizes. From tiny plankton to enormous whales, there's a lot to eat and nearly all of it, living and dead, is used as food. Animals have a variety of adaptations to help them find, catch and eat their food.

What and how an animal eats depends on where it lives and the body parts it has. Fast-swimming fishes like tuna can overtake slower ones like herring. Barnacles live securely attached to rocks by their heads and can't chase prey; their waving, feathery feet catch bits of food that drift in the ocean's currents.

All animals must eat, and all are potential food for other animals. Plants and animals are connected to each other in predator-and-prey relationships called food chains and food webs.

A food chain links predators and prey simply and directly. One food chain in the sea begins with the sun, the energy source for a kelp plant. The kelp plant is eaten by a sea urchin. The sea urchin, in turn, is eaten by a sea otter. The sea otter may be eaten by a shark.

In nature, it's often more complicated. The kelp food chain isn't a single sequence, but is interconnected with other food chains. Rock crabs eat seaweeds, hermit crabs and dead fishes. Sea otters and shorebirds eat the crabs. This complicated network of interlocking food chains is called a food web.

Food chains and webs are sometimes drawn in the shape of a pyramid (called a food pyramid) and divided into levels including producers, primary consumers and secondary consumers.

Otter

Snail
Abalone
Urchin
Mussel

Kelp
Plankton

Producers, or plants, are on the first level. They support the rest of the food web. On the next level are the primary consumers, or herbivores (animals that eat plants). The second-level consumers, or carnivores, are the animals that eat other animals. In terms of mass, there are more producers than herbivores, and more herbivores than carnivores.

The sun collectors

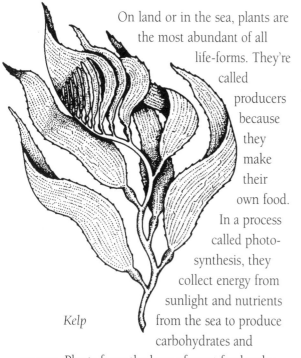

On land or in the sea, plants are the most abundant of all life-forms. They're called producers because they make their own food. In a process called photosynthesis, they collect energy from sunlight and nutrients from the sea to produce carbohydrates and oxygen. Plants form the base of most food webs, and animals ultimately depend on them for food.

Kelp

Flowers, trees and ferns are common plants on land. But what are plants like in the sea? The most common marine plants are algae. Algae that drift in the open sea are mostly tiny plants known as phytoplankton. Phytoplankton are the ocean's most abundant producers. Larger algae, like the 60-foot-tall giant kelp, don't drift; they usually live close to the coast and are called seaweeds.

The plant eaters

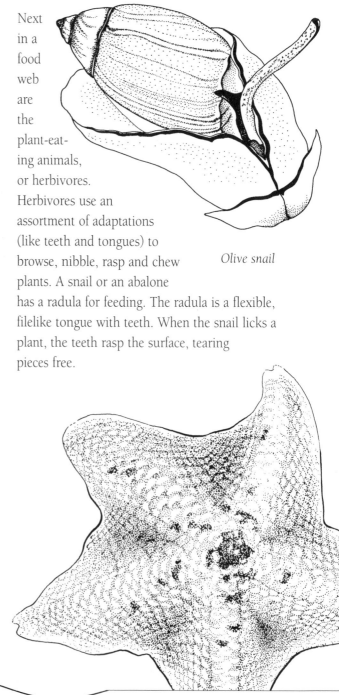

Next in a food web are the plant-eating animals, or herbivores. Herbivores use an assortment of adaptations (like teeth and tongues) to browse, nibble, rasp and chew plants. A snail or an abalone has a radula for feeding. The radula is a flexible, filelike tongue with teeth. When the snail licks a plant, the teeth rasp the surface, tearing pieces free.

Olive snail

Some herbivores are more ferocious than others in the way they feed on plants. Tiny crustaceans, protozoans and larvae (known collectively as zooplankton) gulp down tiny phytoplankton.

Krill

The carnivores

Predators have various adaptations to catch and eat prey. Fast-swimming sharks use sharp teeth to catch and tear fishes and seals. Other animals, like the blue whale, use baleen plates to filter food from the water. They eat up to four tons of shrimplike krill each day.

Sea stars and sea otters both eat animals with hard shells, but have different

ways to get at the tasty morsels inside. The many-armed sea star uses suction cups to open a clam or mussel. It slips its stomach inside the prey's shell, secretes digestive juices and swallows the souplike food. The sea otter collects a rock while foraging for sea urchins and mussels. At the surface, the otter floats on its back and uses the rock as an anvil to crack open the hard shells.

Some animals eat whatever plants and animals come their way.

Abalone and sea otter

Many, like mussels, barnacles and oysters, are filter-feeders. An oyster may strain as much as eight gallons of water an hour for food. Others, like crabs, sea stars and bacteria, eat dead plants and animals and are called scavengers.

Avoiding being eaten

Survival is a balance between eating and avoiding being eaten. Animals have adaptations like hiding, fighting and fleeing to outwit their predators.

Bat star

Tidepool sculpin

Some animals use camouflage. The leafy fins of the kelpfish help it match the colors, shapes and shadows in its kelp forest home. Tidepool sculpins act like rocks, lying very still until the predator has passed.

A sea urchin's spines and a snail's shell help protect them from predators. Some seaweeds and sea slugs produce chemicals that make them taste bad. They're no longer appetizing to an enemy once it's had a taste.

Many fishes swim away quickly to avoid their predators. The fleeing octopus has an added trick; it shoots out a cloud of dark ink and slips away unseen.

People and the food web

Even if you've never visited the ocean, you may be part of an ocean food web. People make ice cream and toothpaste from algae; and they eat fishes, crabs and other invertebrates. Much of our waste eventually finds its way to the sea, where it may get into an ocean food web. Because we share the ocean with plants and animals, we're all part of the same intricate web of life.

Sea urchin

Red octopus

Who Eats Whom?

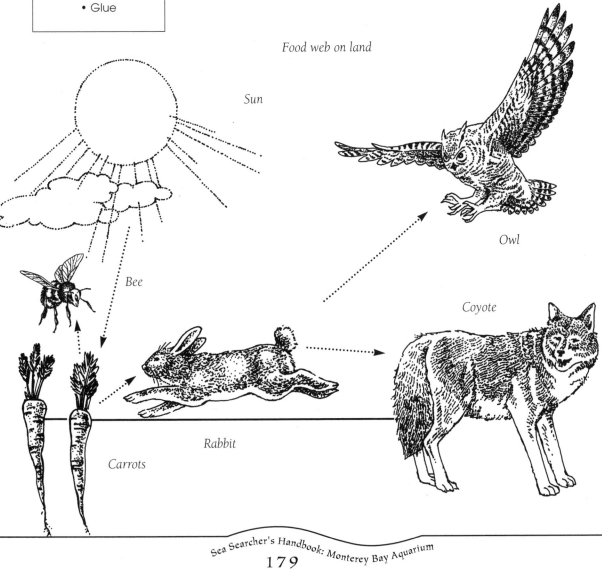

MATERIALS
- Magazines
  Pictures from
  various Field Guides
  in this book
- Paper
- Glue

Create a simple food chain of plants and animals on land using pictures from magazines. You might find a picture of cows eating grass and a grassy field in the sunlight. Now create a food chain of plants and animals in the sea using pictures from the Field Guides in this book. For instance, abalones eat seaweed and seaweed uses sunlight from the sun. Compare your two food chains. How do people fit into these two chains? Can you think of any other members of the food chain (like carnivores, scavengers or decomposers)? What's the difference between a food chain and a food web? (There's more about food chains and webs on pages 175–178.) Turn your food chains into webs.

Food web on land

Sun

Owl

Coyote

Bee

Rabbit

Carrots

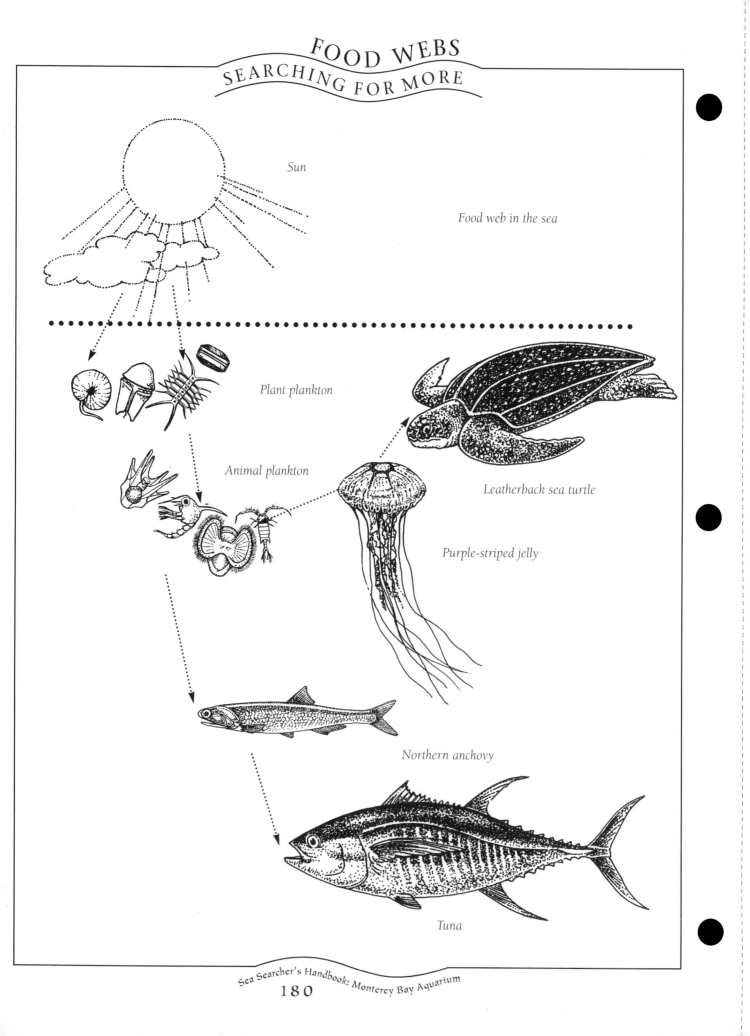

Sun

Food web in the sea

Plant plankton

Animal plankton

Leatherback sea turtle

Purple-striped jelly

Northern anchovy

Tuna

Who Am I?

MATERIALS
• Yourself and friends or family!

Play a fun game of charades with your friends or family. Pick an animal from the sea, then act out how it eats. Have the others try to guess who you are. Can you think of an animal that chases its food?

What's an animal that waits for its meal to come close?

What animals strain tiny plants and animals from the sea?

A shark chases its prey.

Sea Celebration

MATERIALS
- Seafood for a meal
- Cooking utensils

Celebrate a "Taste of the Sea Day!"

With an adult, prepare a seafood meal and invite your friends or family to come enjoy it. Find out what the seafood looks like when it's alive, what part of the ocean it lives in and how it's caught. Share what you've learned as part of your meal!

Sweet to Eat

MATERIALS
- Large sheet of paper or plain tablecloth (make sure you can draw or paint on it)
- Paint and paint brushes or colored pencils
- Toothpicks
- Dried fruits
- Gumdrops and other candies
- Fresh vegetables

Create special sea life that you can eat! Cover a table with a large piece of paper. Color or paint a habitat on the paper. Using a variety of edible foods, design "camouflaged" animals that live on your tablecloth habitat. Which animals are camouflaged best? Invite your friends or family to search for hidden animals, then enjoy eating the ones you find.

Abalone

California halibut

King salmon

SEARCHING FOR INTERACTIONS

People and the Sea

The Sea Is a Special Place

The sea's rich treasures feature sandy beaches, rocky shores, wetlands, kelp forests and deep underwater canyons. Each of these habitats is home to its own thriving community of life—plants and animals uniquely adapted to the physical and biological conditions of their surroundings.

Protected by sanctuaries

In many areas of the United States, National Marine Sanctuaries protect the sea's habitats along with the plants and animals who make their homes there. At the same time, people can use, enjoy and study the sanctuary waters. Activities that could harm the sea's health, like oil drilling, are prohibited. But many others, like fishing and boating, are allowed. Sanctuaries are places where people can experience the wonders of the sea, and know that their children and grandchildren will be able to do the same far into the future.

National Marine Sanctuaries specifically protect the sea and its coastal environment. But this world of the sea doesn't stand on its own. Life here is tied to larger processes like the weather and tides, and to other habitats, including rivers and those on land. Every habitat, every living being—

A wharf piling

including ourselves—is linked to others in a complex tapestry of life. Actions you take at home, even if you live many miles from the coast, can affect life in the sanctuary. It's nature's way.

The sea deserves your care, and needs your help

Since we're part of the sea's web of life, we have a responsibility to help protect it. Below are some of the many ways each of us can help care for the plants, animals, rocks and water—everything that's part of the sea—while at the seashore and at home.

Look closely, step carefully and try not to touch. Most rocks along the coast are covered with living animals. Instead of picking them up, quietly sit and watch for a few minutes. You'll see and learn much more this way.

If you touch an animal, touch it gently. Leave it in its ocean home; many animals die when pried from rocks, and all animals need oxygen from sea water to breathe. Always return animals exactly as you found them; replace any rocks or shells that turn over—they're roofs for many animals.

Use all of your senses. Feel the cool ocean breezes, smell the salty air, listen to the crashing waves.

Tread lightly, and leave the seashore as clean or cleaner than it was when you arrived.

Take pictures—both with your mind and your camera. Leave only footprints in the sand.

Take care at home, too

You can respect and care for the sea as part of your daily life. Remember that much of what goes down your drains and gutters goes out to the ocean.

• Use cleansers that are environmentally safe.

• Recycle your paints and motor oil.

• Buy only the products that you really need and produce as little trash as possible.

Scuba Field Notes

The origins of scuba diving

People have always wondered what lies beneath the waves, and for most of our history, we've looked for ways to satisfy our curiosity. Divers holding their breath (free diving) dipped below the Mediterranean as early as 3000 B.C. to collect sponges and molluscs; Homer's *Iliad* tells of divers in 750 B.C. Sketches from the Middle Ages show that most mechanical devices meant to supply air to divers didn't work. By the late nineteenth century, divers could go below in cumbersome suits and diving bells, with a pumped air supply from the surface.

But it wasn't until World War II that diving was unleashed from air hoses and freed from bulky suits. In 1943, French explorer Jacques Yves Cousteau and engineer Louis Gagnan invented the Aqua-Lung, and scuba (self-contained underwater breathing apparatus) diving was born. Carrying a supply of compressed air on their backs, divers could really stay under water for extended periods and swim about freely, exploring the sea.

Humans as "marine mammals"

Unlike whales, which are naturally well-adapted for ocean diving, humans dive by using artificial adaptations in the form of scuba gear.

Air supply

Even the best free divers can hold their breath for only four to five minutes. Carrying a tank of compressed air, a scuba diver can stay under water for an hour or more. Attached to the air tank is a device that makes breathing underwater almost as easy as breathing on land. Called a regulator, it supplies air at the proper volume and pressure, and only when the diver inhales. As a diver swims deeper, the pressure of the surrounding water grows. It squeezes the lungs, making it harder to breathe. A swimmer breathing through a length of hose in a swimming pool couldn't overcome the added pressure of even two feet of water. The regulator solves this problem; it supplies more and more air as the diver swims deeper and deeper.

Locomotion

Olympic swimmers can churn along at five miles per hour; however, this is a virtual standstill to a whale, which can swim over seven times that speed. Divers use swim fins to improve their performance.

Vision

Because our eyes were designed to focus in air, everything looks blurry when we're under water. A mask solves this by putting a layer of air between a diver's eyes and the water; this makes it look like you're peering into an aquarium. But, as with aquariums, everything a diver sees looks a third larger than it really is. Many a diver, surfacing with what appears to be a large treasure from the deep, has been disappointed to find that it's actually quite ordinary in size.

Body temperature

Water draws heat from the body about 200 times faster than air does. Even warm, tropical waters at 80° F will chill a diver within an hour or two; in the 52° F waters of Monterey Bay, that much time in the water can be fatal unless a diver is protected. In place of the blubber or thick fur that keeps other marine mammals warm, divers use diving suits. A wet suit lets in a thin layer of water, which is then warmed by body heat. The neoprene foam insulates this layer from the cold water outside. Some divers, especially those who dive in very cold waters, use a dry suit that keeps the water out entirely. But even with a well-fitting, good-quality wet or dry suit, Monterey Bay is comfortable for only a few hours at a time.

Buoyancy

Neoprene foam insulates a diver because it is full of tiny air bubbles. For the same reason, it's very buoyant, so a diver must wear 15-30 pounds of lead weights to avoid bobbing like a cork.

Buoyancy changes as a diver goes deeper because pressure compresses the air in the foam. After a certain depth, the lead weights overcompensate for the suit, and the diver begins to sink. To counteract this, the diver wears a buoyancy compensator (an air-filled vest). By blowing air from the scuba tank into this device, or letting air out during ascents, the diver can remain "weightless" at any depth.

In the Kelp Forest exhibit at the Monterey Bay Aquarium, volunteer divers feed fish and clean windows.

Connected to the Sea

> **MATERIALS**
> • Map that shows your home and the sea

Think about how your everyday life relates to the sea. What products from the sea do you use at home? (One of the ingredients in ice cream and toothpaste comes from seaweed.) If you visit the sea, what do you do while you're there?

What kind of impact do you have during your visit? (Boating and picnicking may disturb habitats or the plants and animals that live there; tide poolers may step on and squish tide pool animals.) What happens to water that goes down the drain? Even if you live far from the sea, check a map to find your home, school and local waterways. Are you connected to the sea?

Trash's Trek to the Sea

> **MATERIALS**
> • A map of your local area's storm drain system (available at city hall)

Visit your local city hall to get a map of your area's storm drain system.

Storm drain

Find your home on the map, then trace the path a piece of plastic or a puddle of motor oil takes from your home's storm drain to the sea (or a river or lake).

What are some common ways plastics and motor oil get into storm drains? (Plastics blow off a picnic table or out of a car; oil is poured into drains or gutters.) Design methods to remove plastics or oil from the sea, then send your design ideas to people who make key decisions about keeping the sea a clean, safe place.

How Many Bottles?

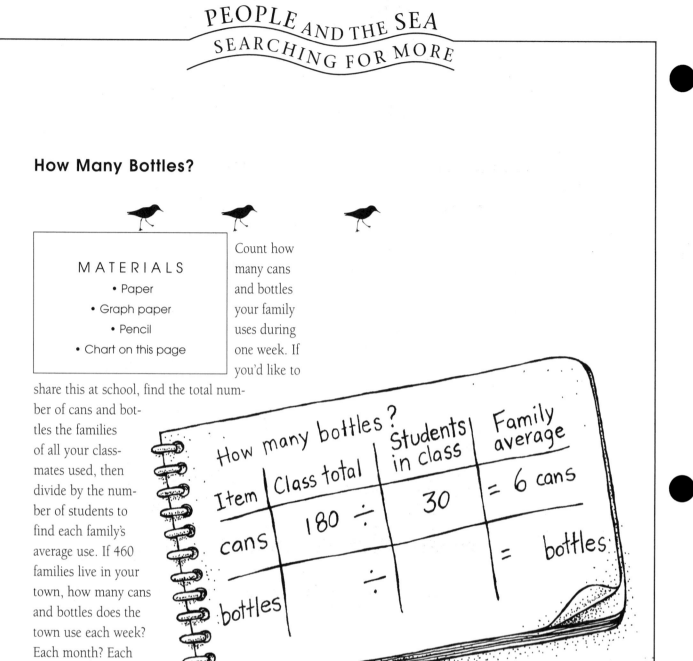

MATERIALS
- Paper
- Graph paper
- Pencil
- Chart on this page

Count how many cans and bottles your family uses during one week. If you'd like to share this at school, find the total number of cans and bottles the families of all your classmates used, then divide by the number of students to find each family's average use. If 460 families live in your town, how many cans and bottles does the town use each week? Each month? Each decade? How much would your town use if each family had one more child? Graph your results. What can you do to use less? Choose three ways and practice them.

How many bottles?

Item	Class total	Students in class	Family average
cans	180 ÷	30	= 6 cans
bottles	÷		= bottles

Less Is Best

MATERIALS
- Cardboard boxes
- Crayons or paints and paint brushes
- Scale
- Chart

How much plastic do you throw away at home? Decorate cardboard boxes to collect plastics for one or two weeks. Weigh your daily plastic use on a scale and record the results on a chart or graph. Share your findings with your family, then challenge them to throw away less. Chart or graph your progress over time.

How do plastics get from your trash can to the sea? (How close is your local dump to a waterway?) What happens to plastics that get to the sea? (Animals have died from eating plastic bags that they thought were jellies; others choke on or are strangled by plastic objects like six-pack rings.) Discuss and list ways people can reduce their use of plastic (like choosing products with little or no plastic packaging, using paper or wax paper bags, reusing bags, recycling and buying less). How much total plastic trash does your family produce each month and year? What is the average amount per person? How much space does one person's annual plastic waste take up? How much space does your family's waste take up? What about the amount of space your town's waste takes up?

Survey your neighborhood to see how much plastic each household uses, or how much waste oil a car produces from an oil change. Develop a presentation or play to show neighbors how plastics or oil get from their home to the sea, how it affects ocean animals and how they can manage and reduce their waste.

THE RECYCLING CLUB

Start a recycling club at home, school or in your neighborhood. Help your school or community center set up or get more people involved in a recycling program. Contact your local waste disposal company to help you.

Planet Earth Test

Give your toys the "Planet Earth Test." How many
of your toys are made from plastic? How many are
packaged in plastic? Could you recycle unused or
broken toys? How? Remember that the next time
you go to the toy store, you can make choices
about your purchases, just like your parents.

*Whenever you can, buy toys and other products
with little or no packaging.*

Finding New Ways

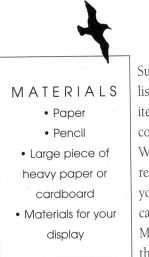

MATERIALS
- Paper
- Pencil
- Large piece of heavy paper or cardboard
- Materials for your display

Survey your home and list all the disposable items (like razors, soap containers and paper). Which ones can you recycle? Which ones can you reuse? Which ones can you use less of? Make a display to show the disposable items that can be recycled and the substitutes that could replace the items that can't be recycled or reused.

A plastic bag can be used a few times, while a plastic container can be used over and over again. The same holds true for paper and cloth napkins, and for disposable and non-disposable razors.

Keep it Clean!

MATERIALS
- Several pans of water
  A selection of materials that can
  pollute water (dirt, leaves, plastics,
  oil, soap, food coloring)
- Various tools to remove pollutants (like strainers, cotton, a stove
  or hot plate for boiling)

Here is a variety of pollutants. Can you think of any more?

Put the different materials in a pan of water, then try various methods (straining, absorbing, boiling) to remove them. Compare which methods work for each pollutant. (Be sure to help younger children with the stove or hot plate.)

Even natural materials like dirt and leaves can cause damage to animals and their homes when used or disposed of improperly.

_Possible tools and methods for
removing pollutants from the water_

What happens
to the sea and
its animals
when these
materials get
into the water?
Who cleans up
the sea? How
do they remove
pollutants from
the sea?

The Cleanest Town

Design a town that produces little or no pollution. What laws would the town have? What businesses would the town need? What kinds of transportation would there be? How would people change their habits at home to pollute less? What laws would you like to have in real life?

MATERIALS
• Paper
• Pencil

Share It!

MATERIALS
- Shoe box or cardboard box
- Variety of arts and crafts materials
- Scissors
- Glue

With your friends or classmates at school, work in groups of four or five to design, develop and build an exhibit about pollution. What would you want to teach others about pollution and the sea? How would you teach it so that others believed what you said and would want to pollute less?

Sing a Song

Write a song (or change the words of an existing song) about pollution to tell people what it is and how they can stop it.

Sea Searcher's Badge

You're a Sea Searcher! And you've earned your badge. Color the badges provided here or design one of your own. Cut it out and wear it proudly, for there is tremendous joy and respect in knowing, loving and caring for the sea.

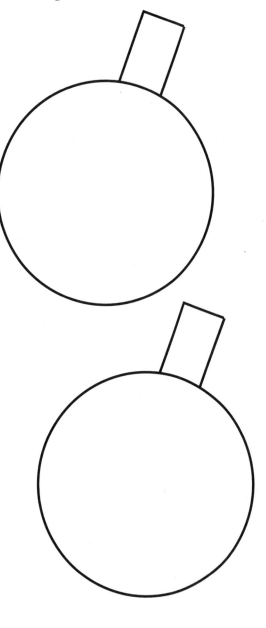

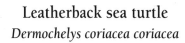

Leatherback sea turtle

Dermochelys coriacea coriacea

SIZE: TO 6 FT. (1.8 M)

Sea turtles eat jellies. When plastic bags and balloons get in the ocean, they look like jellies. Sometimes turtles eat the plastic by mistake, then they choke or starve.

How would you help protect sea turtles?

California sea lion

Zalophus californianus SIZE: TO 7.5 FT. (2.3 M)

Sea lions swim in the ocean. Sometimes they swim into fish nets by accident and get tangled. With a tight net around its neck, a sea lion can't eat.

How would you help protect sea lions?

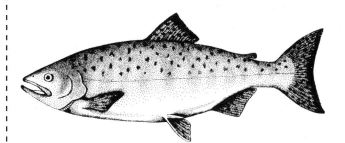

King salmon

Oncorhynchus tshawytscha SIZE: TO 5 FT. (1.5 M)

A salmon spends part of its life in a river. When people dump or spill harmful chemicals into rivers, they poison the salmon that live there.

How would you help protect salmon?

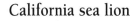

Brown pelican

Pelecanus occidentalis SIZE: TO 7 FT. WINGSPAN (2 M)

A pelican's feathers keep it warm in the cold sea. When a bird swims in an oil spill, its feathers get oily and clump together. An oily pelican that can't keep warm will die.

How would you help protect pelicans?

Pismo clam

Tivela stultorum SIZE: TO 6 IN. (15 CM)

Clams filter water to catch tiny bits of food. Clams get sick if they filter water that's polluted by chemicals or sewage. When people or other animals eat unhealthy clams, they get sick, too.

How would you help protect clams?

People

Homo sapiens SIZE: TO 7.5 FT. (2.3 M)

People are part of the sea's food web. The more people there are, the more fishes we catch and pollution we cause. To help save the sea, we can make careful choices: use less plastic, gasoline and electricity and have small families.

What will you do?

"Conservation is a way of living and an attitude that humanity must adopt if it wants to live decently and permanently on earth."

PAUL BIGELOW SEARS (1891-)
CONSERVATION, PLEASE

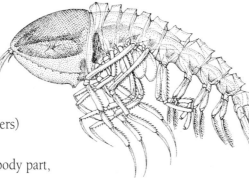

Amphipod

abyssal: deep sea region below 13,000 feet (4,000 meters)

adaptation: a characteristic (body part, behavior, etc.) that helps a plant or animal survive in its environment

algae (singular alga): simple non-seed bearing plants (including one-celled diatoms and multicellular seaweeds)

amphipods: small crustaceans like whale lice, skeleton shrimp and beach fleas

ampullae of Lorenzini: tiny, dotlike sense organs on the snouts and heads of most sharks, skates and rays that can detect electric fields

anadromous: describes an animal that lives in the sea, then swims to fresh water to reproduce

anal fin: a fin on a fish's underside, toward its tail

angling device: a dorsal fin ray or chin barbel on some deep sea fishes that acts like a rod and bait to attract prey or mates

anterior: toward the head or leading end (opposite of posterior)

atmospheric: pressure the pressure of 14.7 pounds per square inch (one atmosphere) exerted by the atmosphere at sea level

baleen: tough, flexible bristles in the mouths of the baleen whales used to filter prey (small fishes, krill) out of water or mud

barbel: a long, slender touch organ extending from the chin of some fishes, sometimes used as a lure to attract prey

bathyal: the deep sea region between 600 and 6,000 feet (183 to 1,830 meters)

benthic: bottom-dwelling; occurring on the bottom of the ocean, lakes, rivers, etc.

bioluminescence: the production of light by a living organism (like the Pacific viperfish's lurelike fin that lights up to attract prey)

blade: the leaflike part of a seaweed

blow: a whale's "spout," or exhaled breath, at the surface of the water

blowhole: a breathing nostril on top of a whale's head

blubber: thick insulating layer of fat beneath the skin of most marine mammals

breach: a whale's leap from the water

buoyancy: an object's ability to float in liquid or air

camouflage: a behavior, shape, color and/or pattern that helps a plant or animal blend in with its surroundings

canopy: the top layer of the kelp forest where fronds float on the sea surface and shade the forest floor

carnivore: an animal that eats the flesh of other animals

cartilage: the tough, flexible tissue (like that at the tip of your nose) that forms the skeletons of some animals like sharks, skates and rays

caudal fin: a fish's tail fin

cetacean: any member of the group (order Cetacea) of marine mammals which includes whales, dolphins and porpoises

chemoreception: the ability to sense chemicals in the environment

claspers: sex organs of male sharks, skates and rays, used to pass sperm to the female

community: all of the plants and animals living in a specific area (habitat); often described by the most abundant or obvious organisms (kelp forest community, mussel bed community, etc.)

competition: interactions between plants or animals in which one adversely affects another for some limited resource (space, food, mates, etc.)

conservation: the practice of protecting nature from loss or damage

consumer: an animal that feeds on other plants and animals

continental shelf: the submerged shelf of land that slopes gradually from the exposed edge of a continent to where the steep drop-off to the deep sea bottom begins

counter-current heat exchange: an adaptation that helps maintain a whale's core body temperature; cooler blood flowing back to the whale's heart recaptures heat from warm blood flowing away from the heart

Bristlemouth

countershading: a type of protective coloration (camouflage) in which an animal is light on the underside and dark on top

crustacean: any member of a taxonomic group of animals which includes crabs, beach hoppers, pill bugs and shrimps

decomposer: an organism, like a bacterium, that causes the decay of dead plant and animal matter

deep scattering layer: a concentrated layer of midwater organisms that can reflect and scatter sound waves produced by sonar devices

deep sea: the deep, lower regions of the ocean where sunlight doesn't penetrate

deposit-feeder: an animal that feeds by consuming detritus on or in the seafloor

dermal denticle: toothlike scales on the body of a shark

detritus: particles from decaying plants and animals

diatoms: microscopic, one-celled algae with silica cell walls

dissolved oxygen: oxygen gas that's mixed in with a fluid like water

diurnal: daily

dorsal: on or toward the back or topside (opposite of ventral)

dorsal fin: a fin on a fish's back

dredge: a net attached to a frame that's dragged along the ocean bottom to collect animals

drift seaweed: a piece of seaweed that has broken free of its attachment and drifts with ocean currents

echo-sounder: a machine that determines water depth by measuring the time it takes for sound waves to reach the bottom and echo back to the surface

echolocation: the use of echoes to navigate or locate prey; sonar used by toothed whales

elasmobranch: a fish (like a shark, skate or ray) with skeleton of cartilage, toothlike scales and no air bladder

Decorator crab

electric organ: cells in the pectoral fins (wings) of some rays and the tails of some skates that release pulses of electricity

electroreception: the ability to sense an electric field, used by sharks, skates and rays to find nearby prey

epipelagic: the upper sunlit ocean layers, to 350 feet (107 meters) deep off central California; also called the photic zone

evolution: the process of gradual change over long periods of time (like birds evolving from reptiles, or the formation of stars, planets, oceans and continents)

extinct: no longer exists

filter-feeder: an animal that eats by filtering or straining small particles of food by passing the water through a filtering device (like barnacle legs, clam gills, etc.)

fish: a vertebrate with scales and fins that lives in water and breathes with gills

flukes: a whale's flat, horizontal tail fins

food chain: a sequence of plants and animals that shows who eats whom; the direction food energy is transferred from one creature to the next, like from the kelp plant to a sea urchin to a sea otter

Sand crab

food pyramid: a food chain in the shape of a pyramid that shows the one-way flow of food energy from the producer(s) up to the consumer(s). There are more producers pound-for-pound at the pyramid's base supporting fewer consumers at the top. The pyramid model shows how energy is lost at each step.

food web: a complex network of interconnected food chains

frond: a kelp stipe and the attached blades

gas bladder: a gas-filled sac found in many fishes that helps provide buoyancy; also called a swimbladder

gill: a respiratory organ where blood vessels absorb oxygen from the water and release carbon dioxide into the water

gill cover: a bony flap that covers and protects the gills; also called an operculum

gill raker: a bony, toothlike structure that keeps food and other solid material from entering the gills

gravity: the force of attraction one body has for another (a property of all matter)

habitat: the place where a plant or animal lives (its home)

hadal: deep sea region below 20,000 feet (6,100 meters); the deep trenches

herbivore: an animal that eats plants or plant matter

hermaphrodite: an animal or plant with both male and female sexual organs

holdfast: the part of a seaweed that attaches it to the seafloor

hydrodynamics: the study of fluids in motion and the movements of objects through fluid

ichthyologist: a person who studies fishes

intertidal: the area of shore between the highest and lowest tide levels

invertebrate: an animal without a backbone

kelp: any of the large brown seaweeds, like *Macrocystis* (giant kelp)

krill: shrimplike crustaceans (mostly of the genus *Euphausia*) to two inches (five centimeters) long; large populations live in certain seas and are the main food of some fishes and baleen whales

larva (plural larvae): the young and immature form of an animal, unlike the adult, that must change to become an adult

Humpback whale

lateral line: a sense organ on some fishes that detects the slightest water movements; a series of tiny pits with hairs that form a visible line along both sides of a fish

light absorption: the dimming of light as it passes through water

Macrocystis: the scientific name of giant kelp

mammal: a warm-blooded animal with hair that breathes air, has internal fertilization and nurses its live-borne young

marine: of the sea

marine snow: organic particles that fall into the deep sea from the sunlit surface layers

melon: a dolphin's or toothed whale's protruding, fat-filled forehead that is used like a lens to focus sounds

mesopelagic: the twilight midwater zone (660 to 3,300 feet [200 to 1,000 meters] deep) between the upper sunlit zone and the dark ocean depths

midwater: the region between the ocean surface and the bottom

migration: an animal's travels from one region to another that occur on a natural cycle, like the steelhead's journey from a river to the ocean and back

minus tide: a low tide below the average lower low ("zero") tide level

mysticete: a baleen whale having baleen mouth parts and two blowholes (like gray whales and blue whales)

neap tide: tides during the quarter- and three-quarter moon when the sun and moon are at right angles (and there is the least difference between high and low tides)

nekton: animals that are active swimmers, like a slender snipe eel, salmon and shark, that are strong enough to move against ocean currents

nictitating membrane: a membrane or eye-lid that extends over a shark's eye to protect it from mechanical injury

oceanography: the study of all aspects of the physics, chemistry, geology and biology of the sea

odontocete: a toothed whale having a single blowhole (like sperm whales, orcas, dolphins and porpoises)

omnivore: an animal that eats other animals and plants

operculum: a bony flap that covers and protects the gills; also called the gill cover

opportunist: an animal that eats almost any plant or animal that comes its way

organism: a living thing, like a plant or animal

parasite: a plant or animal that lives in or on another plant or animal and obtains nourishment from it

Brittle star

pectoral fin: one of a pair of fins along a fish's sides just behind its gills

pelagic: occurring in the open ocean

pelvic fin: one of a pair of fins on a fish's underside, usually just below and behind the pectoral fins

photic zone: the upper sunlit ocean layers to 350 feet (197 meters) deep off central California; also called the epipelagic zone

photophore: a body organ that makes light

photosynthesis: the process by which green plants use energy from sunlight to produce sugar and oxygen from carbon dioxide and water

phytoplankton: plant plankton

pinniped: a member of the group (suborder Pinnipedia) of marine mammals having finlike feet or flippers (like seals and sea lions)

planktivore: an animal that eats plankton

plankton: plants and animals (mostly tiny) that swim weakly, or not at all, and drift with ocean currents

pod: a group of whales swimming closely together

Olive snail

pollution: degradation of the natural environment

posterior: toward the rear or trailing end (opposite of anterior)

predator: an animal that kills and eats other animals

prey: an animal that is killed and eaten by a predator

producers: life forms (plants, diatoms, some bacteria) that produce their own food through photosynthesis

radula: a filelike tongue or band of horny teeth used by snails and most other molluscs to scrape algae, bore into shells, etc.

ray: a fish (related to sharks) that bears live young and has a cartilaginous skeleton, broad flat body and blunt snout

Remotely Operated Vehicle (ROV): an unmanned submersible vehicle used to film and collect deep sea animals

salinity: the salt content of a liquid (sea water salinity is about 3.5 percent)

saltmarsh: community of plants rooted in soils that are alternately flooded and drained by tides

scales: thin, overlapping flat plates that form a protective outer covering on fishes, reptiles and the legs of birds

scavenger: an animal that eats dead plants or animals or their parts

schooling: several to hundreds of fishes swimming together in a very coordinated manner

scrimshaw: decorative carving of walrus tusks and whale teeth and bones

sessile: stationary; attached to the seafloor or an object like a pier piling

sexual dimorphism: a distinct difference in appearance between males and females of the same species (like the smaller size of most male baleen whales)

skate: an egg-laying fish (related to sharks) with a cartilaginous skeleton, broad flat body and pointed snout

slough: a marshland or tidal waterway

sounding: a whale's long, deep dive, usually taken after a series of shallow surface dives

species: plants or animals that are similar to each other and breed only with one another

spiracle: a small gill opening, just behind the eye, in some sharks and all skates and rays

spout: a whale's blow, or exhaled breath, at the surface of the water

spring tides: tides during the new and full moon when the sun, moon and Earth are all in line (and there is the most difference between high and low tides)

spyhopping: the whale's act of raising its head vertically above the water, possibly to look around or navigate by coastline

stipe: the stemlike part of a kelp plant connecting the holdfast to the blades

submarine canyon: a long, narrow, steep-walled undersea valley

submersible: a submarine vehicle used in oceanographic studies

substrate: a surface; the material on/in which an organism lives, like rock, sand, mud, pilings, shells, etc.

subtidal: below the intertidal, or below the level of the lowest tide

California sea lion

surfline: the area near shore where the waves break

suspension-feeder: an animal that filters out detritus or other particles suspended in the water

swimbladder: a gas- or oil-filled sac found in many fishes that helps provide buoyancy

terrestrial: of the land

thermocline: a zone where the temperature drops rapidly as you descend into deeper water

tidal creek: narrow channels that meander through the saltmarsh and are subject to changing tides

tide pool: a pool of water left along the shore as the tide level falls

tide: the daily rise and fall of sea level along a shore

trawl: a funnel-shaped net towed through the ocean to collect fishes and invertebrates

trophic level: a link along the food chain, like producer or primary consumer or secondary consumer

twilight zone: the midwater zone of dim light between the sunlit, photic zone and the completely dark, deeper zones

upwelling: the movement of cold, nutrient-rich waters from the ocean depths up toward the surface layers

ventral: on or toward the belly or underside (opposite of dorsal)

vertebrate: an animal with a backbone

vertical migration: an animal's daily or seasonal movement up toward the ocean surface and back down to deeper water

vestigial: a nonfunctioning remnant of a body part that once existed as a fully functioning part of an animal (like a whale's vestigial hipbones)

whale lice: amphipod parasites on the skin of some baleen whales

wrack: seaweed that has washed up on shore

zonation: the distribution of the plants and animals in a community into recognizable zones

Kelp wrack

zooplankton: animal plankton

> " . . . I would rather sit on a pumpkin
> and have it all to myself,
> then be crowded on a velvet cushion."

HENRY DAVID THOREAU (1817-1862)
WALDEN

Additional Resources Available from:

MONTEREY BAY
AQUARIUM®

Visit the E-Quarium: the Monterey Bay Aquarium online

To learn more about marine life and marine conservation, visit the E-Quarium: the Monterey Bay Aquarium's site on the WWW. Families, teachers and students can browse interactive educational pages, download bibliographies of children's marine life books, peek into the marine habitats of Monterey Bay through online cameras focused on aquarium exhibits. Links to other marine science and education sites will guide you on an online voyage of discovery. Other pages guide you to the aquarium itself; providing all the info you need to plan an aquarium visit.

Just point your browser to: http://www.mbayaq.org

Natural History Series

Richly illustrated with color photographs and watercolors, the books in our natural history series make great reference books for students and amateur naturalists alike. The California Department of Education has listed them in *Recommended Reading Science-Related Literature; Kindergarten through Grade 12.*

Octopus and Squid

James C. Hunt

Discover the amazing variety of octopuses, squids and cuttlefishes that crawl, swim or glide like ghosts in almost every ocean habitat from rocky coasts to the deep sea. Learn new facts, separate truth from fiction and uncover previously unknown behaviors of these animals that have long captured people's imagination and fascination in

Bat ray

this latest volume in our natural history series.
ISBN: 1-878244-16-7. Soft cover, 6^1/$_2$" x 9^1/$_2$", species list and index, 64 pp., $9.95. sku# 47155.

Seals and Sea Lions

David George Gordon

Discover the fascinating lives of these fin-footed marine mammals and explore the adaptations that make them successful survivors in waters from the Arctic to the tropics.
ISBN: 1-878244-06-X. Soft cover, 6^1/$_2$" x 9^1/$_2$", species list and index, 64 pp., $9.95. sku# 23624

Sea Otters

Marianne Riedman

Learn captivating details about these enchanting marine mammals.
ISBN: 1-878244-03-5. Soft cover, 6^1/$_2$" x 9^1/$_2$", index, 80 pp., $9.95. sku# 14746

Sharks and Rays of the Pacific Coast

Ava Ferguson & Gregor Cailliet

Unlock the secrets of these elusive fishes and explore how they live and why they behave the way they do.
ISBN: 1-878244-02-7. Soft cover, 6^1/$_2$" x 9^1/$_2$", species list and index, 64 pp., $9.95. sku# 14745

Gray Whales

David G. Gordon & Alan Baldridge

Join the whales' annual coastal migration from Baja California to the Bering Sea, and share new insights into the behavior of these remarkable long-distance travelers.
ISBN: 1-878244-04-3. Soft cover, 6^1/$_2$" x 9^1/$_2$", index, 64 pp., $9.95. sku# 16515

Seashore Life on Rocky Coasts

Judith Connor

Meet a cast of hundreds who are perfectly adapted to survive the pounding waves, drying sun and shifting tides of the emerald tide pools.
ISBN: 1-878244-05-1. Soft cover, 6^1/$_2$" x 9^1/$_2$", index, 64 pp., $9.95. sku# 18813

Kelp Forests

Judith Connor & Charles Baxter

Explore towering undersea forests that shelter an endless variety of sea life.
ISBN: 1-878244-01-9. Soft cover, 6^1/$_2$" x 9^1/$_2$", species list and index, 64 pp., $9.95. sku# 13717

Elkhorn Slough

Mark Silberstein & Eileen Campbell

Visit this extraordinary coastal wetland which hosts an abundance of bird and marine life.
ISBN: 1-878244-00-0. Soft cover, 6^1/$_2$" x 9^1/$_2$", species list and index, 64 pp., $9.95. sku# 13716

For Young Sea Searchers

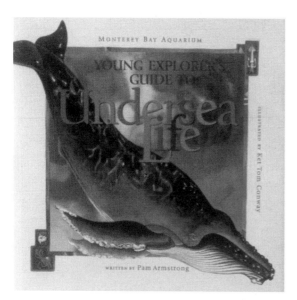

Young Explorer's Guide To Undersea Life

Pam Armstrong
Come meet sea lions, killer whales, humpback whales, elephant seals, leopard sharks and moon jellies—just a few of the many wondrous sea creatures that almost leap off the pages of this book. Colorful borders surround the exquisite watercolors of plants and animals and feature what the animals eat, what eats them or how they live. It's a book of discovery that opens the realm of life in the sea to readers of all ages.
ISBN: 1-878244-10-8. Hard cover, 10$^{1}/_{2}$" x 10$^{3}/_{4}$", 30 full color watercolors, glossary, 64 pp., $16.95. sku# 92508

Sea Life Coloring Book

Deborah A. Coulombe
This coloring book showcases sea life in full-page illustrations and lively, interactive text that invites readers to explore a variety of habitats from rocky coasts to the open ocean.
ISBN: 1-878244-13-2. Soft cover, 8$^{1}/_{2}$" x 11", answer and color key, 16 pp., $3.95. sku# 47104

Flippers & Flukes Marine Mammals Coloring Book

Deborah A. Coulombe
Flippers & Flukes, based on the family/kids exhibit at the Monterey Bay Aquarium, lets kids compare themselves to marine mammals as they color playful images of baby whales, dolphins, seals and sea lions.
ISBN: 1-878244-14-0. Soft cover, 8/2" x 11", color key, 16 pp., $3.95. sku# 47121

Also of Interest

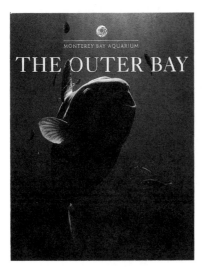

The Outer Bay

Michael Rigsby
A visit to the Outer Bay carries us to the edge of another world. These restless waters are home to translucent, pulsing jellies and sleek, muscular fishes; pastures of microscopic plants and huge whales. Let us guide you through the limitless boundaries of one of the Earth's largest habitats. More than 40 color photographs and illustrations bring the open ocean to life.

ISBN: 1-878244-12-4. Soft cover, 24 pp. $8^{1}/_{4}$" x 11", over 50 fun facts, 24 pp., $5.95. sku# 92491

A Guide to the World of the Jellyfish

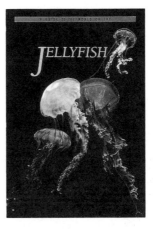

Eileen Campbell
Discover the incredible life histories of these mysterious creatures. More than 40 stunning color photographs and illustrations and lively text bring jellies to life.

ISBN: 1-878244-08-6. Soft cover, $7^{1}/_{2}$" x $10^{3}/_{4}$", 16 pp., $5.95. sku# 17212

Monterey Bay Aquarium

Michael Rigsby
A visitor's guide and more, this souvenir book stands alone as a "window on the bay," showcasing the beauties of one of the world's richest marine environments.

ISBN: 1-878244-07-8. Soft cover, $8^{1}/_{2}$" x11", 48 pp., $6.95. sku# 18503Videos

Videos

Behind-the-Scenes at the Monterey Bay Aquarium

Explore a hidden world few people ever see in this rare behind-the-scenes tour. You'll see all the beautiful exhibits from the visitor's point of view. Then you'll venture into the back with our staff during this 45-minute video. Includes music by John Huling as heard in our internationally acclaimed exhibits.

VHS or Beta format, close captioned, 45 minutes, $24.95. sku# 47172

The Monterey Bay Aquarium Video Treasury

Bring the best of the aquarium into your classroom! Dr. Steven K. Webster, director of the aquarium's Education Division for over ten years, introduces 10 of the aquarium's best exhibit videos. Discover the kelp forest, submarine canyon, rocky shore and open sea . . . Learn about whales, sea otters, seals and sea lions, plankton, squid and other appealing characters in Monterey Bay . . . join an aquarium collecting expedition.

VHS format, 69 minutes, $24.95. sku# 12815

Jellies and Other Ocean Drifters

Venture into the vast, fluid realm of jellies and other ocean drifters. From the restless, sunlit surface waters to the dark, cold and mysterious depths of the deep sea far below, the ocean is home to strange and wondrous creatures. Narrated by Leonard Nimoy, you'll see breathtaking images of delicate jellies trailing long tentacles, predatory comb jellies, web-weaving larvaceans, colonial salps and 30-foot-long siphonophores. Lyrical music sweeps us along on their journey, as we explore a seldom-seen world.

VHS or Beta format, 35 minutes, $19.95. sku# 22964

How to Order

TRADE, WHOLESALERS AND LIBRARIES

Books (except for *The Outer Bay*) are available through our distributor
ROBERTS RINEHART PUBLISHERS.
(800) 352-1985
Videos and *The Outer Bay* may be ordered directly from the Monterey Bay Aquarium Gift and Bookstore.

INDIVIDUALS

You may order books and videos directly from the aquarium by calling our Gift and Bookstore.
MONTEREY BAY AQUARIUM
Gift and Bookstore
(408) 648-4952

Join A Group Working to Protect the Sea

American Oceans Campaign

American Oceans Campaign is a national nonprofit organization dedicated to protecting America's marine ecosystems and drinking water supplies by educating the public through science, the media, advocacy and coalition-building.

725 Arizona Avenue, Suite 102
Santa Monica, California 90401
PHONE: (310) 576-6162
FAX: (310) 576-6170

Center for Marine Conservation

The Center for Marine Conservation, a national nonprofit organization, seeks to conserve the diversity and abundance of ocean life through citizen action, science-based advocacy and the promotion of sound conservation policies.

1725 DeSales Street, NW
Washington, D.C. 20036
PHONE: (202) 429-5609
FAX: (202) 872-0619
E-MAIL: dccmc@ix.netcom.com
WEB SITE: http://www.cmc-ocean.org

Friends of the Sea Otter

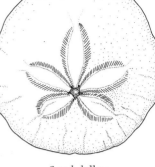

Sand dollar

Friends of the Sea Otter (FSO) is a not-for-profit organization founded in 1968 dedicated to the protection of a rare and threatened species, the southern sea otter, as well as sea otters throughout their north Pacific range, and all sea otter habitats.

2150 Garden Road, B-4
Monterey, California 93940
PHONE: (408) 373-2747
FAX: (408) 373-2749
E-MAIL: Fndseaottr@aol.com

The Marine Mammal Center

The Marine Mammal Center rescues and rehabilitates ill or injured marine mammals; returns healthy animals to the wild; conducts research; and educates the public on our marine environment and its critical importance to the health and survival of all life.

The Marin Headlands
Golden Gate National Recreation Area
Sausalito, California 94965
PHONE: (415) 289-SEAL
FAX: (415) 289-7333
E-MAIL: members@tmmc.org
WEB SITE: http://www.tmmc.org/

Monterey Bay Aquarium

The Monterey Bay Aquarium, a nonprofit institution, seeks to stimulate interest, increase knowledge and promote stewardship of Monterey Bay and the world's ocean environment through exhibits, education and research.

886 Cannery Row
Monterey, California 93940
PHONE: (408) 648-4880; (800) 840-4880
FAX: (408) 648-4810
E-MAIL: cclark@mbayaq.org
WEB SITE: http://www.mbayaq.org/

National Audubon Society Living Oceans Program

The National Audubon Society's Living Oceans Program mission is to restore abundant marine wildlife and healthy habitats in our oceans and along our coasts.

Dr. Carl Safina or Mercedes Lee
550 South Bay Avenue
Islip, New York 11751
PHONE: (516) 224-3669
E-MAIL: mlee@audubon.org

The Nature Conservancy of California

The Nature Conservancy's mission is to ensure the preservation of the full spectrum of California's natural diversity by protecting biologically sustainable ecosystems, exemplary natural communities and threatened animals and plants.

201 Mission Street, 4th Floor
San Francisco, California 94105
PHONE: (415) 777-0487
FAX: (415) 777-0244

Save Our Shores Marine Sanctuary Center

The Save Our Shores mission is to protect the ecological integrity of the Monterey Bay National Marine Sanctuary through policy research, education and citizen action.

2222 East Cliff Drive, Suite 5
Santa Cruz, California 95061
PHONE: (408) 462-5660
FAX: (408) 462-6070
E-MAIL: SaveOShore@AOL.COM

Surfrider Foundation

The Surfrider Foundation's grassroots environmental organization is dedicated to the protection of coastal waters, waves and beaches.

122 S. El Camino Real #67
San Clemente, California 92672
PHONE: (714) 492-8170 (800) 743-SURF
FAX: (714) 492-8142

World Wildlife Fund

World Wildlife Fund works worldwide to preserve the abundance and diversity of life on Earth and, through its marine program, focuses on three strategies: restoring critically threatened fisheries; reducing pollutants that endanger marine life; and promoting integrated coastal management, including marine protected areas.

1250 24th Street, NW
Washington, DC 20037
PHONE: (202) 293-4800
FAX: (202) 293-9211
E-MAIL: eichbaum+r%wwfus@mcimail.com

Northern elephant seals

Together we can care for and protect the sea,
today and in the future.

ILLUSTRATION CREDITS:

Carlson, Kirsten/Monterey Bay Aquarium: 160 (top right)

Caudle, Ann/Monterey Bay Aquarium: front & back cover, title page, 1, 3, 4, 14, 29, 44, 61, 75, 88, 109, 110, 121, 145, 157, 173, 174, 184, 202, 215 (school of anchovies, bat ray, purple-striped jelly, kelp, thresher shark, red octopus)

Cruttenden, Carla: iv, 15, 16 (top), 17 (1st row, top right; 2nd row; 3rd row, bottom left and center; 4th row, bottom left), 20 (top left [crab] & bottom), 25 (top & center), 26, 27 (bottom), 28, 32 (top), 36 (right center), 52 (top left), 66 (bottom), 72 (bottom), 74 (top), 115 (top), 119 (bottom), 120 (top & bottom), 130 (top), 155 (top), 175 (middle row: top left, bottom left & right), 176 (bottom), 177 (bottom), 178 (top & center),

Duke, Larry/Monterey Bay Aquarium: 131

Eyre, Randi/Monterey Bay Aquarium: 10 (top), 11-13, 20 (top), 21 (center), 22, 23, 34, 35, 36 (top left), 52 (right column, 3rd and 5th from top; left column, 2nd & 5th from top), 56 (bottom), 65, 66 (top right), 67, 80 (bottom right & left), 81, 82 (top), 94-96, 98, 114, 115 (center), 116, 117, 118, 132, 134, 135 (bottom), 150 (right), 151, 152, 161 (bottom), 162-164, 179, 180 (top left), 181, 182, 186, 189-197, 200 (bottom)

Faust, Ann/Monterey Bay Aquarium: 100, 180 (center [anchovy])

Folkens, Pieter A./Monterey Bay Aquarium: 122 (bottom)

Kells, Valerie/Monterey Bay Aquarium: ii, vi, vii, 5, 6 (bottom), 7 (top), 8 (top), 9, 17 (4th row, bottom right), 21 (bottom), 36 (bottom), 45 (bottom), 47, 49-51, 52 (left column, 3rd & 4th from top), 53, 57 (center), 58, 59 (bottom), 62, 66 (bottom left), 70, 71, 72 (top & center), 73 (top & center), 77, 78, 82 (bottom), 86 (bottom), 87 (center), 89 (bottom), 90-93, 97 (bottom left), 99, 103, 104, 105 (top & bottom), 106, 111, 113, 125, 129, 130 (bottom), 137 (bottom), 141 (center), 142 (top), 143 (top), 144 (top & center), 146, 147, 150 (left), 153 (top), 155 (center & bottom), 156 (top), 159, 165 (top), 166 (top), 170 (bottom), 175 (top row; middle row, top right), 177 (top right & left, center), 180 (center right & bottom), 183 (top & bottom), 185, 187, 188, 198 (bottom right), 204-206, 208, 209, 217

King, Jane/Monterey Bay Aquarium: 6 (top), 16 (bottom), 17 (1st row, top left), 25 (bottom), 27 (top), 30, 31, 32 (bottom), 33, 38, 40-43, 52 (top right & bottom left), 59 (top), 60 (bottom), 76 (bottom), 79, 80, 86 (top), 87 (bottom center), 119 (top), 122 (top), 123 (bottom), 124, 128, 135 (top), 137 (center), 140 (center & bottom), 141 (top & bottom), 142 (top & center), 143 (center & bottom), 144 (bottom), 175 (bottom right), 176 (top right), 178 (bottom), 180 (left center), 199 (center), 200 (center), 207, 209, 210-212, 221, 223

Kopp, Kathy/Monterey Bay Aquarium: iii, 10 (bottom), 48 (top), 52 (right column, 2nd from top & bottom), 55, 57 (bottom), 66 (right center), 112 (bottom), 119 (center), 123 (top), 126 (bottom), 127, 133, 136, 138, 139, 140 (top), 148-149, 153 (center & bottom), 156 (center & bottom), 176 (center left), 183 (center), 199 (bottom), 200 (top)

McCann, Andrea/Monterey Bay Aquarium: front & back cover, title page, 1, 3, 4, 14, 29, 44, 61, 75, 88, 109, 110, 121, 145, 157, 173, 174, 184, 202, 215 (brown pelican), v, 7 (bottom), 48 (bottom), 52 (right column, 4th from top), 54, 56 (top), 59 (center), 60 (top & center), 63, 87 (bottom), 97 (bottom right), 105 (center), 165 (center & bottom), 166 (bottom), 198 (bottom right)

Monterey Bay Aquarium: 18, 19, 39, 45 (top), 68, 69, 76 (top), 85, 86 (bottom), 89 (top), 101, 102, 126 (top), 180 (top right), 199 (top)

Packard, Julie/Monterey Bay Aquarium: 175 (bottom left)

Stein, Mike/Monterey Bay Aquarium: 24, 46, 57 (top), 158, 160 (top left & bottom), 161 (top), 166 (center), 167-169, 170 (top & center)

Thompson, Frances: front & back cover, title page, 1, 3, 4, 14, 29, 44, 61, 75, 88, 109, 110, 121, 145, 157, 173, 174, 184, 202, 215 (rock crab, bat star, red abalone, brown turban snail, red urchin), 17 (3rd row, right; 4th row, center), 27 (center), 64, 73 (bottom), 74 (center & bottom), 112 (top), 120 (center)

REFERENCES:

Belt, Thomas. (1991). *Introduction to The Naturalist in Nicaragua.* In J. K. Terres (Ed.), *Things Precious & Wild: A Book of Nature Quotations* (p. 25). Golden, CO: Fulcrum Publishing. (Original work published in 1928.)

Carson, Rachel. (1956). *The Sense of Wonder* (p. 42). New York: Harper & Row, Publishers.

Emerson, Ralph Waldo. (1991). *Literary Ethics.* In J. K. Terres (Ed.), Things Precious & Wild: A Book of Nature Quotations (p. 83). Golden, CO: Fulcrum Publishing.

Sears, Paul Bigelow. (1991). *Conservation, Please.* In J. K. Terres (Ed.), *Things Precious & Wild: A Book of Nature Quotations* (p. 164). Golden, CO: Fulcrum Publishing. (Original pamphlet issued by The Women's Garden Club of America.)

Thoreau, Henry David. (1991). *Walden.* In J. K. Terres (Ed.), Things *Precious & Wild: A Book of Nature Quotations* (p. 204). Golden, CO: Fulcrum Publishing. (Original work published in 1942.)